Fridays with Jim

DAVID COHEN

Fridays with Jim

Conversations about our country with Jim Bolger

MASSEY UNIVERSITY PRESS

Introduction 7

Wexford 23

Taranaki 49

The Altar 77

Church 89

Wellington 115

Ninth Floor 141

Armageddon 193

Washington 211

Waikanae 237

Afterword 277

Acknowledgements 282

About the Author 283

Index 284

Contents

Introduction

The idea for putting together a collection of conversational interludes with Jim Bolger came to me a couple of years ago, when I was researching a story about New Zealand's diplomatic and trade history. Part of the brief had involved taking an hour's drive north from my home in Wellington to the coastal town of Waikanae to spend a Friday morning with the man who had been our country's thirty-fifth prime minister.

I felt that, as a former political leader, corporate player and a one-time ambassador, he could deliver some insightful comments. This he did with familiar aplomb.

Familiar *is* the word, too. Jim — pardon the deviation from usual journalistic style rules, but this is a first-name-basis book — is now in his mid-eighties. It's as if he has always been with us.

Oh sure, these days the hair is more vividly white. Those pale blue eyes have now acquired a more benign look. And, yes, he occasionally slips into referring to himself in the third person, in a slightly more crackly voice than that youngish new Cabinet minister used in the late 1970s and early 1980s. But the Bolger gusto, always one of his great signatures, is still there. See him out mowing the lawns or gardening in the large section he shares with Joan. Listen to him holding forth on one or other of his pet themes — the eclipse of the white global class, say, or the environment — and there's no doubting the energy level.

Yet something else that struck me at the time was how little has been published over the decades about the actual man. It's a surprising omission: Jim Bolger has been in the public eye on and off for the past half-century, most notably as a three-term prime minister, and yet we don't know him and his interesting paradoxes all that well. A man from an orthodox party who is yet not an orthodox thinker. A quintessentially New Zealand leader from a relatively unusual background among New Zealand chiefs. A business leader who has moved in the wealthiest circles yet comes from an economically tough personal background. An academic leader who dropped out of school early. Appearances to the contrary notwithstanding, he's never really been a status quo kind of guy.

You'd think we would already have all that good oil. Actually, not so. The basic details of that public life are well known, and en route to the pantheon of political trivia. Any winning team in a pub quiz could tell you, for instance, that James Brendan Bolger, the son of Irish immigrants, was born in the Taranaki village of Opunake in 1935. His parents farmed rock-strewn land. He left school early to help them. Later, he married a young teacher, Joan Riddell; started his own family; and bought a sheep and beef farm in the King Country. The couple would eventually have nine children.

Unsurprisingly, he became involved with Federated Farmers, which was to be the springboard for a political career. He entered Parliament in 1972 as the National MP for the newly created seat of King Country. Three years on, the Opposition surged into office.

For most people of a certain age, Jim came to prominence as a minister of labour serving under Robert Muldoon. It was an era in

If only catching votes was so easy.

which the country sizzled with industrial disputes; at any one time there were as many as 30 roiling the economy. Compulsory unionism, which Jim would later be instrumental in dismantling, was the order of the day for workers. In an appointment that would probably be considered odd by today's standards, he was also an undersecretary for Maori Affairs.

The advent of television was pivotal to his political ascendance. Norman Kirk, whose one-term Labour government Muldoon had toppled in 1975, was the first New Zealand politician to really use the medium, and Muldoon later made it his own. Jim had neither the screen power of his leader nor Kirk's oratorical flair, but he looked appealing enough, and his background in debating was (and still is) an advantage.

Most strikingly, according to historian and former Labour minister Michael Bassett, he could be fearless when the occasion demanded, as much in Parliament as he had been when representing farmers. 'While extolling the virtues of his constituency, he revealed a sense of history, and understood the inevitability of change,' Bassett has noted. 'That kind of perception is not always the hallmark of farmers.' Nor, Bassett also noted, was he reluctant to break with tradition; despite the convention that new MPs should give only light and frothy maiden speeches, in 1972 he used his to launch a spirited attack on the newly elected government of Norman Kirk.

Jim became leader of the National Party in 1986. In the first few years he had the opportunity to study the relatively brief premiership of Geoffrey Palmer and the ridiculously briefer one of Mike Moore. Taking notes came naturally to somebody who, according to his former press secretary, Jim Burns, 'undoubtedly made mistakes, but never made the same mistake twice'.

No doubt part of Jim's success story was the dire state the Labour government found itself in by the late 1980s. Its economic reforms had proved a mixed blessing at best. Squabbles and ideological ructions were rife. This all helped National secure its largest ever victory in the 1990 election, but so too, obviously, did its turbo-charged leader who, despite never doing wonderfully well in the public opinion polls, ticked off all or most of Michael Bassett's seven essential attributes for leadership: high ambitions, rude good health, intelligence, good [self-] education, the ability to come across well on television, a supportive home environment, a cheerful temperament, the capacity to make tough decisions and, perhaps most importantly, the ability to give a sense of a better world.

Among the achievements of Jim's stewardship of the country as prime minister was the introduction of a mixed member proportional (MMP) representation system. He helped negotiate a number of pioneering Treaty of Waitangi settlements, including with Ngāi Tahu and Tainui. He persuaded his party to embrace Labour's signature anti-nuclear policy and, most critically, his government brought the country's accounts back into balance. He nudged New Zealand's perception of itself away from being a satellite of Europe and towards being a fully fledged member of the Asia–Pacific region.

Considerably less successful were his attempts to promote republicanism, an argument he made on local terms rather than on the Irish experience that informed his conviction. Although, here again, good instincts possibly saved him from going out on a limb as the party's next three-term leader, John Key, did on the flag issue, and pushing for a referendum he could not possibly hope to carry.

In 1990 National was elected on the promise of delivering a 'decent society' but would be known for delivering what many regarded as a decidedly indecent Budget, a famously austere one delivered by Jim's right-hand-woman, finance minister Ruth Richardson. Her 1991 Budget slashed government spending, which was arguably needed, while also undermining the softer brand National had been trying to project in the wake of the right-wing economic policies of the previous ninth-floor crowd. This was something the new government did not need.

Jim and his finance minister eventually parted company. Later still, in 1997, Jim would have his own parting of ways with his caucus when a confident Jenny Shipley deposed him as leader. It was the first successful coup against a sitting PM in decades — and ultimately one of the most pointless. Two years later the party was dispatched by Helen Clark's impressively re-energised Labour Party. It took National another three elections and four more leaders before they won again with John Key.

The man Shipley got rid of might, understandably, have percolated in bitterness over this. Apparently not so. There followed a successful dive into diplomacy as New Zealand's ambassador to Washington. Jim held this position for four years, most dramatically as our man in the American capital on the morning of 11 September 2001. He has since held a number of corporate positions, including, recently, a 12-year stint as chancellor of the University of Waikato, a ceremonial but influential role. His chairmanship of several boards has included being founding chair of Kiwibank and of the country's renationalised rail operation, KiwiRail.

Most of this stuff is relatively easy to find from a quick computer search. It's harder to discover anything much else offering a personal vantage. If, as Michael Bassett says, the real keys to Jim Bolger's life have been his rude good health, his religion, his marriage, his good temperament and a bit of (Irish) luck, then little has been written about any of this. I know it hasn't because I looked for it two years ago. I looked for it again before raising the subject with Jim.

This book tries to fill that gap.

This wasn't the first time I had thought about the missing Bolger narrative. In a sense, our Friday morning sessions actually began when I first met Jim back in July 1989, when he was prepping for what would be a successful campaign in the following year's general election. I was prepping for my own journalistic career by getting into the habit of interviewing political leaders.

The first of those interviews was with Jim's one-time political boss, the sourpuss of Tāmaki. I was in my early twenties, and more than a tad nervous as I presented my tape recorder to Rob Muldoon. Although he was no longer the country's premier, the old warrior still enjoyed a reputation for chewing up cub reporters. And there he was, in the moody light of yet another far-flung Friday morning, all red-rimmed eyes and rollicking mouth. No formalities, no hellos. In the event, Muldoon was relatively good-humoured, which was just as well because my tape recorder broke down about five minutes into the interview and we had to reschedule.

I interviewed most of the Labour leaders (and even got sued by one). Later there was Jenny Shipley, who had recently completed her transition from Sunday school teacher to being the woman who ended Jim Bolger's premiership. That was interesting. Lists of the many things she passionately believed in filled many pages of my notebook. Otherwise, I mainly stuck to pressing the record button. I remember wishing she didn't spend so much of her time smiling.

I also interviewed Jim a number of times. The first was that earlier piece for the *Evening Post*, then again later while he was PM, and once more with feeling in Washington DC, where we sat together in the monastic hush of his office at the New Zealand embassy. At the time of our first encounter, and indeed for a good period afterwards, the Labour Party was short of breath. This provided a natural angle for my original article. Afterwards, I remember thinking I should have made more in the piece about his obviously impressive knack for sensing the popular mood. This was something that was starting to be reflected in the polls.

His farming background probably had something to do with it. Certainly, it must have given him the constitution he obviously needed to keep the business ticking over while also raising nine children and discharging his political duties. It has also made him a recognisable Kiwi type. And growing up in a small rural community gave him a gut feel for what that average New Zealander might be thinking or feeling; even as he has always insisted, perhaps not entirely convincingly, that he is somewhat impervious to popular fashion and mood.

The more I reflected on it, the more I perceived a number of other themes in his life with which I hazily felt some degree of personal identification, or at least keen interest. Take his lack of formal education. Jim is one of four premiers during my lifetime who quit school early — he was 15. The other three were Keith Holyoake, Norman Kirk and Mike Moore, which, when you think about it, says something about our country. Something good, I think.

It has often occurred to me in journalism that the better the formal education most people have, the more entangled (for lack of a better word) in it they tend to be, even decades after they get their diplomas or degrees. At first — and here I speak as one drawn from the ranks of the autodidactic — I used to rather envy this and wish I could have been part of that self-contained, socially advantaged elite. Gradually I changed that view. I started to appreciate that my kind of educational experience had the great benefit of leaving no trace on me at all. Any academic deficiencies are more than compensated for by the fact that one's first experience of adult life comes not through a cloistered education by people from exactly the same environment but rather by people actually living and earning their living.

Jim is an example of what I mean. Here's a self-taught man who learnt the ropes in the real world and went on to run a government for the better part of a decade with the corporate touch of a Harvard MBA — and no, the Ivy League comparison isn't strained. More than one old parliamentary hound I chatted with made a point of saying that the Bolger-style executive branch of the 1990s was the country's first truly professionalised political structure.

The self-education probably explains other things about him, not least his much commented on, and sometimes derided, knack for mimicking accents, which might come more naturally to people who take their lessons from those they are talking with, and a slightly overformal way of speaking. It probably also says something about his pragmatic sensibility. When you learn your cues by listening to others, it's natural to make room for at least some of their arguments. He also grew up quite poor by today's standards. That's hardly surprising for the offspring of migrants from Wexford, Ireland, who arrived in New Zealand with little money and who started out in this country as farm workers during the straitened height of the Depression.

Jim's commitments during his formative years also meant he never got to experience the Kiwi rite of passage, the great OE, until he was a slip of a lad of 63. I refer, of course, to his successful stint as the country's ambassador to Washington DC. Here our paths crossed again when I interviewed him for *Metro*, the now defunct Auckland city magazine.

Finally, there was the world as it is today, on which the country's oldest elder statesman seemed well placed to offer thoughtful views. And who isn't interested in that?

Oh, I nearly forgot to mention Covid-19. Actually, Jim was the first to mention it. Around the time we wrapped up our conversations, in early 2020, we were chatting about the likely production schedule for the book. I mentioned that I thought it would probably be printed in China.

'That could be difficult,' he murmured.

I didn't understand what he was getting at, and so he explained: the coronavirus. I scratched my head. I had only vaguely heard of it, and had assumed it was just another strain of the flu making its way around parts of East Asia.

'Oh, this is going to be big,' he said warmly. 'Really big.'

So much for my prognosticatory powers.

The weeks went on. The news got worse. Naturally, the question arose as to whether we should include an additional conversation about the subject that had quickly absorbed everyone on the planet. Yet it would not have been all that straightforward.

Part of the problem was that the general understanding of the new virus was changing by the day. We knew everything about it, and we knew nothing about it. We didn't know definitively when it started, precisely where it began or how it was circulating. In light of all this, the only thing that seemed sure was that anything Jim had to say about the condition would date badly — possibly by the following week, let alone by later in the year.

A few days after our initial exchange on it, however, he gave what in retrospect appears to have been a prescient speech in Waikanae, to members of Zone Four of Local Government New Zealand, touching on what was then still a nascent menace:

> The biggest immediate threat in the world at the moment is the coronavirus, which was first identified in Wuhan in China. And the

A Jim Hubbard cartoon from 2001.

first big lesson that the virus has reinforced is how interconnected today's world is and so every day the virus has spread further. There are the obvious upfront personal and community health risks and associated costs. The amount is as yet unknown, but very large financial costs across the world are inevitable.

China is New Zealand's largest export market and that means New Zealand will suffer significant direct financial costs as most industry sectors will be affected. The bigger issue, as the virus spreads, is its impact on the world economy and whether the spread and the measures taken to control the virus will drive a world overburdened by debt into recession.

These costs will range from food exports through to Chinese students being unable to come to New Zealand to study. Education is our fifth largest export earner.

Other costs will be related mainly to the export sector like food, timber and tourism. Tourism will be a big upfront loser, but the losses will flow on to virtually all other sectors. Collectively we can expect a virus that first appeared on the other side of the world to significantly impact our economy.

And on it went, segueing from the new virus to the speaker's politically passionate views on climate change. Voila! We had a superbly fitting conclusion. This has therefore been added as a book-end, and it is one of a number of hard-to-find (on the internet at least) speeches by Jim over the years that have been sprinkled throughout the text. Later, as we communicated over the finished project during the national lockdown, Jim and I agreed that we should probably update the text with a bit more on the damn virus. Those updates have been dotted in here and there, along with a fresh aside on the political ascension of his one-time staffer Todd Muller.

Elsewhere, the book sticks with the personal themes I originally picked out, around which we structured a year-long series of monthly conversations in Waikanae. Usually we met on Friday mornings. The idea was always less to present a biographical portrait than a collection of revealing interludes drawn from 30 or so hours of conversation.

The chapters have all had a bit of editorial intercession, mainly in the interests of excising repetition, or adding in the odd corrected fact here and there, but the text is still basically as it happened. In all but the last chapter, my voice has been dropped from the text, mainly because the question and answer format can become wearying to read over the long haul. I did go back to that format in the final chapter because it was more conversational than thematic.

The title of this book, *Fridays with Jim*, is a bit of a play on Mitch Albom's celebrated memoir, *Tuesdays with Morrie*, about a series of visits the American author made to his old sociology professor, who was dying of motor neuron disease. But there the similarity ends. As readers will, I hope, enjoyably discover for themselves, our great helmsman is very much alive.

Wexford

James Brendan Bolger. Jim. Almost everybody calls him Jim; they did so even during the years he was prime minister. Certainly, no one called him Sir. Jim, of course, is a well-known (and unknighted) republican who believes New Zealand is quite capable of standing on its own two feet. What observers sometimes don't immediately get is the connection between the former prime minister's staunch views on this front and his Irish roots.

Yet each of these two facts casts the biggest shadow on the other and is in turn shadowed by the other — and if that sounds like a surprisingly Irish way of putting it, that's sort of my point in turning the first of our conversations to this theme.

For all the talk one sometimes hears, often after a couple of glasses of wine, about New Zealand's Anglo-Celtic character, our country has always leant a bit more to the Anglo side in respect of its dominant cultural style. Here I'm drawing on some personal experience. My own mother arrived in New Zealand from Carlow, a small Irish town located less than an hour away from Wexford, which just happens to be from where Jim Bolger's farmer parents emigrated.

Historically, whether in the case of Daniel and Cecilia Bolger in 1930, or my mother three decades on, newcomers from the Emerald Isle have tended to feel the pressure to conform to this other cultural norm. That's hardly surprising, given that most of the great waves of Irish immigrants went to North America and of the much smaller number who made it to our part of the world, most ended up in Australia.

There's a reason. According to New Zealand historian Jock Phillips, writing on the magnificent Te Ara website, in peopling its settlements the New Zealand Company excluded Irish peasants from the assisted passages on offer. Hardly any of the company's settlers were therefore Irish-born. And those who were tended to be from a wealthy Anglo-Irish background — which is to say, Anglicans who came here in part because they fretted over the emergence of Irish nationalism. Very early on in our history of Pākehā settlement there were very few Irish: in 1848, for example, there were just 175 Irish souls in Wellington and the entire South Island.

You can see the same absence in the fledgling New Zealand political establishment. The country's ninth premier, Daniel Pollen, was a Dubliner, but his term in office lasted only a matter of months. A couple of other leaders of Irish stock both hailed from Ulster. The only other leader with immediate family roots in the Republic of Ireland to manage the economy for any serious length of time remains Jim Bolger.

Ireland seemed like a good place to start. Besides, I had just got back to Wellington from a week in Dublin, and I was dead keen to talk about the family ties that bind.

So let's start the story. In 1930 my parents, Daniel Bolger and Cecilia Doyle, then aged 32 and 28, made a six-week journey across the known world from County Wexford, Ireland, to a country, New Zealand, that they knew virtually nothing about. That decision displayed a confidence in their ability to overcome whatever obstacles they might confront in their new homeland. Whatever way I look at it, it was a brave decision, driven perhaps in part by necessity but more certainly by the desire to make a better future for themselves and their as yet unknown family. I am proud of them.

In Ireland their family homes were about 20 miles from where US President John F. Kennedy's family had come generations before. The story of that county, the cornerstone of Ireland's ancient east, is interesting however you look at it, and it's important, too, because I don't think we can ever escape our history, at least in some ways. And the Irish, of course, know nothing if not their history.

An uncle on my mother's side, Dennis Doyle, was a raconteur of this history, and of poetry. I wish I could always remember poetry like that. Most of the Irish can talk, too, which has certainly been my experience with my own relatives. Irish history, which has been difficult over the centuries, offers a lot to talk about. The various visits we've made there over the decades have enabled both of us — Joan's been with me on every visit — to understand where the Irish perspectives come from, and in part have helped explain why the Irish are scattered across the world.

So much history, so much of it troubled and complex. Of course, it was in one form or another a virtual colony of England for most of its modern history — by which I mean the last 800 years. But its cultural origins go back at least 10 times as far, 10,000 years or perhaps even more, since the first known people arrived in Ireland; amid Wexford's naturally dramatic landscapes there's rich evidence of human habitation going back to the Bronze Age and even earlier.

Wexford also has other claims to fame. It has been the seat of uprisings and rebellions, most notably the one in 1798 that's still recalled and lamented in Irish folklore. In modern terms — again, if you can call 200 years ago modern — this constituted one of the great campaigns against English rule. And Wexford would also be the setting in which that ambition was put to the military test, going right up until 1922.

Virtually anybody from the county can talk authoritatively about all this, and accompanying that authority is a still-raw sensitivity. I was reminded of this in 1998, shortly after I stepped down from being prime minister and was en route to Washington to take up my new post as New Zealand's ambassador there. Earlier that year I had been invited to speak at the final bicentenary gathering at the medieval Wexford Castle to recall the 1798 uprising against English rule. In talking with a cousin I learnt that there had been some debate within the community about whether a 'foreigner' should be giving this extremely sensitive Wexford speech.

So when I spoke I reached back into New Zealand's own sensitive history, to our Māori people and the concept of tūrangawaewae, or knowing where you come from. Which of course confers a right to return and to speak on the marae if the occasion so warrants. I reminded the audience that the bones of my ancestors lie in Wexford and therefore I claimed my right to speak. This went down really well. I also remember from that visit the way they go through all the great battles of the past, including the final battle, which was just outside the ancient town of Enniscorthy, on a modest rise called Vinegar Hill. I've been there many times. It overlooks the low rolling flat lands and is where the rebels lost that final battle and so rule from London continued for another 124 years, until 1922.

Let's move forward from the defeat in 1798, which cost many lives, including members of the Doyle and Bolger families. The desire for freedom and a free and independent Ireland did not diminish. It was carried forward in song and story. It wasn't that much later, in the 1840s, that there was a terrible famine caused by the potato blight which destroyed the potato crops of Ireland. That famine scarred a whole generation, and successive generations, too.

Out of a total population of about six million, around one million people died, on the streets, in the fields and everywhere else, from actual starvation even as their English landlords were exporting food, using confiscated land to produce it. The famine, in turn, led to an exodus of about two million, primarily to the United States, but really across the world, leaving the remaining population decimated, angry and distraught. It also set the scene for the Land War, which was followed by the return of the potato blight to Ireland, all of which boosted nationalism, republicanism and, of course, emigration and misery.

Eventually, we know, London did start to send some grain in, but it was often inedible. The populace subsisted on a little food and a lot of anger. Then you had a pause until the Easter Rising in Dublin in 1916. But that, too, didn't start in a day. The ringleaders of the Easter Rising, 16 of them, were hanged, except for Eamon de Valera, who escaped because he was New York-born and therefore an American citizen. He was sent to jail. He was released two or three years later and went on to serve several terms as the head of government and also head of the independent Irish state.

The republican tide flowed on. From 1916 let's go to 1922, and the decision of London to divide Ireland, granting independence to 26 counties but keeping the six northern counties, which also happened to be the wealthiest six counties, under London's rule. That occurred because they had established the shipyards around Belfast and had brought over a lot of Scottish workers, who happened to be Presbyterians, to work in them. Back then there was little tolerance for different interpretation of the Christian message, so London effectively divided Ireland along religious lines.

Fortunately the Good Friday Agreement signed in 1998 ended most of the violence in Northern Ireland. A divided Ireland has been a major issue in seeking to decide how to have a sensible border between the UK — which includes Northern Ireland — which since Brexit has left the European Union, and the Republic of Ireland, which is a member of the European Union. The only sensible solution is to allow Ireland to reunite and then the border can be the Irish Sea. I believe that will happen.

Back in 1922, the debate in Ireland was intense as to whether Ireland should accept independence minus the six counties. The Irish were divided on that, but even so the then leader Michael Collins went to London and signed and for his trouble was ambushed and assassinated shortly after returning home. This led to a civil war, the aftermath of which created an Ireland divided along political lines between those who were on one side or the other during the fighting. Those were the major political parties in Ireland. In other countries divisions were on the grounds of economic ideologies or whatever. In Ireland it was all about loyalties.

For all that, or maybe because of that, my parents, Daniel and Cecilia, didn't speak much about all this history. I surmise it was all too painful and raw, but perhaps more important in their thinking was that they had moved to the other side of the world and didn't want to burden their family with Ireland's troubled history. I read and heard about it later. My parents did not indoctrinate their children with a dislike of the English. It wasn't an issue at all in our household. They were here in New Zealand and getting on with their lives. They didn't instil a great history of Ireland into their children or talk about why they, or indeed anyone, would leave the vanguard of Irish republicanism for the most English of former English colonies.

Why did they come to New Zealand and not somewhere else? I don't have an answer for that. They were both from very large families. There were 15 in my father's family, and his parents died when he was eight. Whether they both died at the same time, I'm not certain, but they died young. His older sisters brought him up. My mother was one of 12. They were a more substantial farming family, the Doyles, a name that goes back a long way in Ireland, and they had a modest but not insignificant farming property. They're still farming it and still farming around Wexford.

Actually, Wexford has more Doyles, a name of Norse origin, than Israel has Cohens, I think — it's an extremely common name there, as well as in places like Dublin, Wicklow, Cork and Carlow. Here's a story. You're driving down an Irish road with a cousin and he'll say, 'Oh, who it be here? That'd be Johnny Doyle over there, eh, he's a third cousin.' And then you'll drive back the other way with another cousin and he'll say, 'Ooh, it'd be Johnny Doyle over there. But he's nothing to us, of course.'

I was really struck by the place when I first visited after I was appointed minister of fisheries in 1977. New Zealand had a very modest fishing industry at that time, but as the new minister I was keen to develop the industry, especially as the world was discussing the introduction of 200-mile exclusive fishing zone agreements. On that model, and given the location of the Chathams, approximately 400 miles from New Zealand, we would end up with the fourth largest fishing zone in the world, stretching 600 miles out from our east coast.

I proposed to Rob Muldoon that I go on a six-week tour to a number of countries with large and successful fishing industries so that I and my officials could get a general overview of the industry. I have to say that when I was prime minister I never considered letting any of my ministers go away for more than two weeks, and I'm sure Jacinda Ardern wouldn't either, but Muldoon agreed. We started in San Diego, where a large tuna fishing operation was based. From there it was on to Halifax, Nova Scotia, Hull in England and then the former Yugoslavia.

Our discussions in Moscow were important, given the size of the Russian fleet that came down to fish in the south-west Pacific. Alexander Ishkov, minister of fisheries, had held that position since the 1930s. Given the many upheavals in the USSR during that time he must have had highly tuned political skills to have lasted that long. He and his excellent Russian interpreter, Natasha, travelled with the New Zealand party for all of our stay in the Soviet Union. After meetings in Moscow we flew to Khabarovsk in south-eastern Russian. We overnighted there and Ishkov and I had a fishing competition before boarding the Trans-Siberian Railway for a 17-hour journey to the coastal city of Nakhodka. I have to put it on the record that Minister Ishkov won.

At Nakhodka, the base for Russia's large Pacific fishing fleet,

Jim planting an Irish oak at his mother's family home in Wexford on his visit as prime minister in 1993.

I noticed that the large fish processing plant we visited wasn't operating because the power supply was out, and that virtually all the heavy machinery being used to rebuild the port was from Japan, and I wondered whether this was an early indication that the old Soviet system was failing. Japan was our next stop. Given Japan then fished extensively across what would be our new zone, they were very keen to know how they might be licensed to fish in it. The last stop was South Korea, which had a large boat building industry supplying their fishing industry. I realised that for New Zealand to harvest our soon-to-be zone we would need a very big increase in our fishing fleet.

International agreement was reached on the principle of countries having 200-mile exclusive fishing zones and New Zealand's then foreign minister Brian Talboys and I worked on the legislation, which was passed in 1978. That long journey across the world was the beginning of New Zealand's now successful fishing industry and for me it was also an opportunity, as a person who had travelled very little, to get an upfront and close engagement with major countries and senior ministers, which was all very valuable to me at the start of my ministerial career.

Let me now go back to Ireland. After completing bilateral discussions in Dublin, we met up with two of my father's brothers and their families in Dublin. The brothers, Brian and John, had established their own menswear store in the city, and that was where my father was working shortly before setting sail for New Zealand.

We then moved for the weekend down to County Wexford to meet other family members, mainly on my mother's side. When we were down in Wexford I thought of my brother John's eldest son, Peter, who had been killed in a car accident when he was a teenager. Peter never looked much like any of the rest of us but at a gathering in Wexford, I looked across the room and there was somebody almost in his exact likeness. He was Jim Doyle, a first cousin, and Jim became the one who visited New Zealand the most and whom we see at least as frequently as anyone else. I enjoyed meeting my cousins for the first time, both in rural Wexford and in the town of Enniscorthy, which is where we normally stay now with a first cousin, Mick Doyle, and his wife, Ann. Wonderful hosts.

If you go right back on my mother's side, there seems to be more information, including about the number of Doyles who lost their lives in the uprising in 1798. Did that influence my parents? It certainly registers in the family stories that relatives tell. But in 1930, for reasons to which I don't have a clear answer — and I've checked my siblings and neither do they — my parents decided to come to New Zealand. They had to pay their way. They weren't assisted immigrants. Why New Zealand, not somewhere else, was a mystery that died with them.

But necessity must have been a big factor — the need to be somewhere else. My father, who was born in 1898, was then aged 32. Two of his brothers had left Ireland. One, my namesake, another Jim Bolger, who became a significant figure in the railroad business, was in Canada. Another brother, Edward, went to what was then the British Gold Coast, now Ghana, and stayed there for 24 years. He came out to New Zealand in 1949 and ended up farming and I helped him for many weeks one spring. He was single and had no family, and nor did the uncle in Canada. Their parents — my paternal grandparents, John and Winifred Bolger — had little money. When they died, it appears there wasn't enough money to have a gravestone. The location of their grave is registered in the churchyard where they're buried, but there is still no headstone there.

At the time of her marriage, my mother had been looking after the house for her brother Michael, who at that point was single and had bought another farm in a village called Monaseed, which is often a gathering place for us when we go over to Ireland. My mother's parents are buried in the cemetery beside the church in Monaseed.

They set sail for New Zealand, via England, after marrying in the church at Killinierin. I visited that church when I went back to Ireland as prime minister in 1993 and there I met an old man who had been the altar server at their wedding. We had a good chat with him and the local priest, which delayed the evening mass that day. The morning after their wedding my parents took the ferry across to Southampton and from there they were en route to New Zealand. The passage took six weeks.

There's a photograph of them taken at the port of Fremantle, in Western Australia, when they got off the boat. They told us that they were sick of travelling at that point and thought about stopping their journey there, but then they thought, well, they'd paid their fare all the way to New Zealand, and you wouldn't want to waste that money, would you?

It was a long voyage. You can see why people back then usually only made it once. There was something full and final about it. It was the end of your direct relationship with your family and the land of your birth. You knew it was a one-way trip.

In my parents' case, they were married one day and gone the next. Why so quickly? I don't know. Presumably they decided the voyage would be their honeymoon, as it were, and just kept on sailing — to a country where they knew no one, and in the middle of the Great Depression, to boot. You ask yourself — well, I ask myself — how *bad* were things in Ireland at that stage that they decided that a country on the far side of the world was where they should be?

I've often thought about this. If you have the courage to get on a boat and go all that distance to somewhere you don't know, you also have the courage to be confident you can survive that and prosper. That had to be at the back of their minds — or maybe in the front of their minds, more correctly: they were going to do better in a new land. It was sheer optimism, since they knew little or nothing about it, but they must have been sure that they could do better in New Zealand than in the old land of Ireland, their homeland.

But I suppose Ireland prepped them for that, too. The Irish were used to being second-class citizens in their own land. In fact, it wasn't considered their land at all. It was English, and English landlords had virtually all of it. And those terrible events I mentioned had happened within 50 years of their births. It must surely have been a topic of conversation when they were growing up: who had lost who, how many children had died, who had migrated to America, and so forth. Or at least that's what I imagine. I've tried to put myself into their mindset and the mindset of Ireland at that stage. I think it's helped me understand the sense of desperation that some Māori felt in New Zealand, where their land had been taken from them.

They arrived in Wellington in November 1930. They thought they were coming to a warmer place, but there was a hailstorm on the first morning. Then they hopped on a train for Taranaki, to Stratford, where I think there may have been a priest who had been recommended as a contact.

In Taranaki, they got a job hand-milking cows, which was fortunate in an era of very high unemployment. I don't believe my mother had ever hand-milked a cow in her life before that. She always credited the generosity of Jack McHardy, the farmer they worked for

— she never called him other than Mr McHardy — who gave them their first job in New Zealand. I recall asking my mother once how they got the job and she said she had once asked Mr McHardy that question and his answer was because they looked a 'decent couple'.

According to Google, the McHardys were 'the product of an old Highland clan and Catholic Irish stock'. The McHardys had a daughter and two sons, who both became priests. Father Emmet, who died when he was only 28, had been a missionary in the northern Solomons for a few years but had to return to New Zealand when he contracted malaria and TB. He clearly made a lasting impact in the Solomons because when I visited well over 50 years later as a government minister and brought up his name, a number of people could tell me stories about him. Clearly they were impressed by him. His brother, Father John, was a teacher in Marist schools.

My parents were on the McHardy farm for five years. The first three of their five children were born while they were working with the McHardys. That was Daniel and Cecilia's start: hand-milking cows, a little cottage that had no running water, just a cold water tap outside. It was rugged. For many years my mother sewed all her dresses by hand. Then the children arrived, five of us in reasonably quick order. I'm in the middle of the five. A brother and sister on either side. How should I describe our living conditions on the McHardy farm? Spartan is probably the right word. Frontier-like? Certainly. Today's society would be *horrified*. We'd be having a parliamentary commission looking at the standard of the accommodation. But I'm sure that there were many others with similar conditions.

My parents gave their all to the new country. On the war effort, for instance, I don't think they took any other view than a New Zealand one. But as it happened, my father wasn't called up: he was married with five children by then and had a farm and so he was exempt. He

Daniel and Cecilia Bolger at Freemantle, Western Australia, in 1930 during their journey to New Zealand.

was in the Home Guard, which was, by all the accounts I've heard, often quite farcical. They had few weapons to train with and paraded around with broom handles. Sort of like *Dad's Army*. We were living about three miles from the reserve boundary of Mount Taranaki/ Mount Egmont National Park at this point, and the Home Guard men would go up there and do some bush training. All very noble, but the execution was perhaps less than marvellous.

Speaking of things Irish, though, here's an interesting sidebar. Three important figures in New Zealand's political history were Irish born. The first was John Ballance, who was born in Ulster, in County Antrim, and who led the parliamentary movement to give votes to women. He died in April 1893. The law to give votes to women was passed that September, so he unfortunately never lived to see it. Then there was Thomas Bracken, who wrote the words of 'God Defend New Zealand'. And there was William Hobson, the first governor of New Zealand, who was born in Waterford, Ireland, and was Anglo-Irish.

My instinct tells me that my parents wouldn't have been greatly aware of the pedigree of these Irish political figures, because they had become status quo figures by the time they arrived.

Anyway, if you include me, that's a few Irish, and politics was part of the family mix. Perhaps that's how I grew up with a view on things as well. My mother had *many* views, not least on the political life of the day. That carried through to the keen interest my father took in the American election of 1960, when John F. Kennedy was running for president. We had a good shortwave radio which could pick up *Voice of America* and my father would listen to its coverage of the election. Don't forget that the Kennedys lived about 20 miles down the road from the Bolgers. Jack Kennedy, 'a boy from Wexford', was one of *our boys*. Or such was my father's view.

Bubbling under the media coverage of that election, of course, was the big argument over Catholicism and politics, which was of particular interest at the time and would have some personal relevance for me, too. Quite a large lot of commentators said the Americans would never vote in an Irish Catholic as president, and some in New Zealand said something similar. I do recall a journalist around the time that I was emerging in the National Party, and was being spoken of as a potential leader, writing that the party would never accept an Irish Catholic as their leader. Well, I don't think it ever was a factor at all. Or it must have been in deep cover if it was. But nobody ever suggested that to me and I just didn't believe it. In fact, I was totally dismissive of it.

I mean, yes, during the challenging debates on abortion and homosexuality a few years back, people sort of prejudged where you would sit on the issues, as they may have with Bill English and many others — there's a number of Catholics in Parliament now, after all. We tend to prejudge others. We'll prejudge a Catholic to vote one way, but equally prejudge others who aren't Catholic who may vote another way. So it goes on, across the board. Unfortunately, many spend more time prejudging than listening.

In America the subject of Catholics in politics went back a lot further. There was a four-term governor of New York who went by the totally non-Irish name of Al Smith, but who also happened to be the son of an Irish mother. He became the first Catholic to make a tilt at the American presidency in 1928. He was totally demolished by the Republican Herbert Hoover, and thereafter the conventional wisdom was that somebody of Irish Catholic descent could not possibly be elected president of the United States. But then Kennedy came along and disproved that.

After the Kennedy assassination, his vice president, Lyndon B. Johnson, became leader. His first big challenge was on the issue of race, votes and civil rights. I remember the discussions well, including whether Johnson could get the Civil Rights Act passed more easily than Kennedy might have, mainly because Johnson was a more Machiavellian manager of the US Congress. What most people don't know is that in order to get the Senate to agree, the civil rights supporters in the Senate had to overcome an 83-day filibuster by Southern conservatives. Nowadays you would call them Southern Republicans, but at that time they were Democrats from the American South — the 'Dixiecrats' — who were opposed to giving black Americans civil rights.

This all took place against the backdrop of the 1857 *Dred Scott v Sandford* decision handed down by the US Supreme Court, which, if memory serves, was passed by seven votes to two, and basically held that no black man or the descendant of a black man could enjoy the rights of American citizenship. This wasn't ancient history. Still isn't. When you look at America today it's not hard to see why there are problems. It's so ingrained. This perspective helped me to take an entirely different view when dealing with Māori issues than many people in the National Party and across New Zealand might have wanted.

Another aside. I can remember where I was when John Kennedy was shot. Very clearly. I was in the cowshed on the farm at Rahotu, scrubbing down the yard, and it came over the radio in the cowshed. Given who we were as a family, and given that my father had become emotionally engaged in Kennedy's victory, it was a substantial shock. I wasn't watching American politics very much at that stage and I would've known little of the violent gun culture that's such an extraordinary blot on that society. In the years ahead, it was gun violence closer to home that would take up a lot more of my attention.

Address to the Senate

Wexford, Ireland, 31 May 1998

In the 200 years since the rising in May 1798, there has been endless weeping, both real and emotional, as the people of Ireland fought to gain their independence, and so stand tall in their own land.

In the custom of the Māori people in New Zealand, the right to stand and speak on an important occasion is dependent on genealogy, on lineage that connects you to a place, to what they describe as your tūrangawaewae, where you can stand without being challenged to voice your own thoughts and to state your own views. The symbolism of that concept struck me as I accepted the generous invitation to speak at the historic reconvening of the Senate of Wexford, because this is my tūrangawaewae, where the bones of my ancestors are buried.

Your generous invitation also imposed a considerable obligation on me to draw on the strands of half-forgotten memories to recall the thoughts and stories, noble and sad, of the Irish who left Ireland. I am not speaking as one steeped in the agony of Irish history, but as a friend with some knowledge and feeling for all that is Irish.

I speak from the perspective of a New Zealander where the Irish, Catholic or otherwise, are a significant but minority group in our community. The connections between Ireland and New Zealand are many. In 1798 the six-year-old son of a barrister in County Waterford would have paid no attention to the unfolding tragedy in Wexford, and yet that young lad, William Hobson, would, after service in the British Navy, arrive in Waitangi in the beautiful Bay of Islands on the northern coast of New Zealand as the first lieutenant governor of the colony, and on the 6th of February 1840, sign on behalf of the British Crown the Treaty of Waitangi — the treaty between the Crown and the Māori chiefs as gathered at Waitangi. That treaty is today acknowledged as the founding document of New Zealand.

In that same year a royal charter divided New Zealand into three provinces: the North Island was New Ulster, the South Island, New Munster, and the tiny Stewart Island, New Leinster. And so they were known for the next few years. Effectively, the first premier was one Edward William Stafford, an Anglo-Irishman born in Edinburgh, but brought up south of Dundalk. He arrived in New Zealand in 1843, and 13 years later, aged but 37 years, he commenced the first of his three terms as premier. The youngest person ever to hold the position. The anthem we sing, 'God Defend New Zealand', was penned by one Thomas Bracken, born in 1843 in County Meath. His hymn, for that's what it is, was published in 1876, but was not adopted as our official anthem for another 101 years, in 1977.

Men and women in all walks of life, Catholic and Protestant, have travelled from Ireland to New Zealand and every other corner of the world. Wherever they went they contributed to their adopted country in all fields of endeavour and have often risen to the highest office in their chosen careers. They also took with them their love of music, laughter and debate and a passionate interest in people and politics. They did not forget Ireland or its history, or the fact that throughout history Irishmen and -women were often cruelly discriminated against not because of what they had done, but because of what they stood for, because of what they thought, because of what their conscience dictated. Those of Irish descent in far-off New Zealand understood and debated such matters with passion. They understood the moral dilemma of deciding between the dictates of a person's conscience and the dictates of the law. It's moral conflicts of that nature which would have troubled the sons and daughters of Wexford in the lead up to the rising of '98.

Such dilemmas would have weighed heavily on the mind of Father

John Murphy. In anguish he and others felt compelled to respond to the call of the downtrodden, to respond to an unsatisfied yearning for a better social structure where a person was not judged by their religion or their status. That magical call for liberty had echoed through the generations; it appealed to a mystique inaccessible to reason, it encouraged men and women to rise up against impossible odds.

But that was not the only legacy of '98. For me the extraordinary thing that happened in 1798 was not courage on the field or heroism in battle — for that was a given handed down from generation to generation — but that in the midst of the heat and passion of battle the fragile seed of democracy was planted in soil made rich by the bones of those who had died in pursuit of liberty. This morning we joined together in an ecumenical service to pray in the words of the song 'Boolavogue', that heaven's gates opened wide to all those who died in '98, and from that prayer for those gone, we have now moved to this place, this Senate, for it was the Senate of 1798 that embodied a dream that surpassed all others.

This was not a battle for a hilltop, a victory over the redcoats on the field. This was no passing fancy, success to be measured by who killed the most of the opposing force. This was an ideal splendid in its simplicity, stark in its beauty, the ideal that men and women of different traditions respect one another as people, each unique and each created in the image and likeness of God.

This was not simply a battle for home, it was a battle for the then elusive ideal of democracy, where everyone's home would be safe. The ideal was for a senate, a concept that has come down from ancient Rome, to be established in Wexford, where differences could be resolved with words, where the future could be debated between equals. In the Senate they knew that the noblest aspirations of the people of Wexford and Ireland would find expression.

It was here that the great gift of the Irish to paint the future landscape of Ireland with words of emotion, power and poetry would be undertaken. In its safety, embraced by its civilising influence, warm in its security, great dreams of the future could be given voice.

Leaders and people from the four winds of the Irish diaspora acknowledge that dream today. For that dream did not die on Vinegar Hill. It did not die with the death of Father Murphy. It is the dream of repressed people the world over. Today we recall and pay tribute to the extraordinary moral courage of those visionaries who in 1798 saw the new future for this land, not through battle, but through tolerance. Visionaries who understood that tolerance implies no weakness or lack of commitment to one's beliefs; rather that tolerance condemns oppression and persecution of others for their beliefs.

A man of the twentieth century I admire and love, and am proud to call a friend, is Nelson Mandela. It was he who said that his ideal of a non-racial, democratic South Africa was an ideal he was prepared to die for. His punishment was not death but 27 long years in prison but he emerged not embittered and seeking revenge, but seeking tolerance so as to build a new and better South Africa.

I shared with thousands that wonderful day of his inauguration as the first black president of his nation. I was moved by his hope that 'Out of the experience of an extraordinary human disaster that has lasted too long, must be born a society of which all humanity will be proud.' I say as a visitor who loves his Irish heritage that that same ambition must inspire the thinking of all those gathered in this Senate and across Ireland today.

The human disaster of division, bloodshed and bitterness in Ireland has lasted too long. Nine days ago, 200 years on from Wexford, by democratic voice the people of the island of Ireland voted in overwhelming numbers for a new constitutional framework to embrace this land of saints and scholars. The 'yes' vote so eagerly sought must be used to build a society, which Irishmen and -women from all traditions can be proud.

Two hundred years on, the heirs of 1798 see a different Ireland. I see before me a vibrant nation which is reaching out to the world in all fields of endeavour. A prosperous nation in Europe whose sons and daughters no longer of necessity must leave home to seek work and opportunity. Instead Ireland is now known for the export of its commerce, its literature and its arts. Its music and dancing give joy to the world. This can be the generation that will reach the promised land of religious and political liberty by openly accepting differences in tradition, practice and belief.

Every country, including my own, has history they are not proud of; events happened which cannot be justified, we all have memories that are painful, but as we approach the door of a new century let us do so with a warm heart, a willingness to forgive and a willingness to embrace our neighbours whoever they may be. Let that door to the future be big enough for all in Ireland to walk through together. That is the Ireland the founders of the original Senate hoped for, that is what Wolfe Tone spoke out for, that 'all people are free and equal in rights'. The Irish have surely paid in full the price to achieve that ideal.

As we gather in this reconvened Senate and recall the visionaries and heroes of the last 200 years I express my hope that all communities in Ireland commit themselves in their hearts to a community of Ireland where Irish orators will no longer feel compelled to 'call on the sacrifice of the dead to justify the sacrifice of the living'.

Achieve that and you will have achieved the towering ambition of those who founded the Senate in Wexford in 1798, and so with optimism I farewell those from both traditions who fought for liberty.

Moe rai te ringa kaha o Atua. Rest in the strong hand of God.

Taranaki

It is by no means true that those who have the best formal education are the most interesting, witty or successful subjects. Indeed, the opposite is sometimes true. Just ask Jim Bolger — which is what I spent our early Friday mornings doing.

Time was, and not so long ago, that higher education was strictly a minority pursuit anyway, not least in the ruling class. In the 1960s, Keith Holyoake startled a visiting British diplomat by boasting that, in the words of one biographer, 'He was no intellectual, he was not well educated, he left school when he was 14, and had never been near a university.' Holyoake wasn't the only one. As Jim points out, Norman Kirk quit his studies even earlier, and Mike Moore bolted from the classroom around the same age. It's really only since the time of David Lange that degrees started to become run of the political mill.

New Zealand isn't alone in this. David Lloyd George, Winston Churchill, James Callaghan and John Major were all British prime ministers who never attended university. Churchill had the advantage of going to Harrow, I suppose, which was effectively a university-level academic experience, but the others attended fairly ordinary schools and nothing else.

I like the fact our country has been flexible enough to accommodate leaders with the best scholastic pedigree along with those who learnt their chops on the road, as it were. But if I had to choose between doing a study of one or the other, I would definitely go for the latter, and that's not just a whimsical feeling. People are often a little more interesting when their background is slightly out of the conventional educational focus. The edges are a bit more blurred. It's never pinchbeck.

Significantly, perhaps, many well-known organisations, including Apple, Google, IBM and the *Spectator* magazine, have all dropped the need for job applicants to have formal qualifications. Why? Because these are often the people whose different experiences have given them the kind of different minds that these places might need. So are they correct? Does it matter anyway? These seemed like matters that the man who went on to become University of Waikato chancellor might be nudged to chat about while reflecting on his own formative years.

I was born at Opunake Cottage Hospital on the coast, 40 miles south-west of New Plymouth. By the time I started school we were on a small farm my parents had bought in Omata. According to the latest census, these days Omata and its surrounds have a population of just 540. Omata was where I spent my first year at school. Many years later as prime minister I went back to help the local school celebrate its 125th anniversary.

My memory of the family farm in Omata is a bit ragged on specifics, but I think it was 60 acres. Lots of gorse, a very old house and shed, and a terrific pear tree. My older brother John and I used to round up the cows that had strayed into the neighbours' properties because the fences were so poor. My parents presumably decided buying that farm had been a mistake, so in 1941 we moved to Rahotu, further south down the Taranaki coast, where they had bought 94 acres. The farm was very typical of that part of coastal Taranaki: there was virtually no flat land and its hills were full of rocks from eruptions from Mount Taranaki, and it was difficult to farm because of the small swamps and creeks that criss-crossed the land. My brothers and I, number two shovels in hand, grew up helping to drain those swamps.

Years later, when my father died suddenly of cancer in 1962, I bought the family farm with the help of a State Advances Corporation loan. I was 27. Joan and I were married in 1963 and in 1965 we sold the farm at Rahotu and bought a modest sheep and beef farm at Te Kuiti. We developed that farm and over the years added to it by the purchase of additional land. The Te Kuiti farm is now part-owned and managed by our son Stephen and his wife, Toni.

The Rahotu farm had been part of the farm resettlement scheme after World War I. The house was relatively new and sound, but it was small and had none of those things that modern houses have: the toilet was outdoors, there was a coal range in the kitchen, and a copper to boil the water in the laundry-cum-bathroom. There were three bedrooms and a kitchen/dining space as well as a small lounge. Obviously there was no shower: the bathroom only had a bath and a sink. The telephone arrived many years later.

It was modest, and there were definitely wealthier farmers than the Bolgers. We were near the bottom end of the scale in those terms. Our transport was an old Nash car that had been converted into a small pick-up truck. If all the family needed to go somewhere like church on Sundays there would be three in the cab and four on the back, irrespective of the weather. I don't recall our financial position impacting on me, and perhaps that's because I was a confident young fellow and it didn't bother me. I think there would have been a universal acceptance in the district that the Bolgers were hard workers. My mother, with help from her children, would often have the job of milking the cows, especially for the evening milking. My father was also an extraordinarily hard worker on this rundown farm, where we milked only 28 cows at the start. It's interesting that a family could live, even if very modestly, on so few cows in 1941. I can recall when we got to 30. We had arrived at the farm in the era before tractors.

I can still remember the work my father did digging big, wide drains by hand. One of the neighbours once came over to look at what he was doing and, impressed, asked whether he was going to sail the *Queen Mary* up them.

The land was on what were known as West Coast Settlement Reserve Leases. This was Māori leasehold land that was established following the colonial government's confiscation of land from Taranaki Māori after the invasion of Parihaka in 1881. The government then decided they'd taken too much so they gave some back to Māori. Well, that's my interpretation. The land was put under 999-year leasehold titles, which were perpetually renewable, and so to all intents and purposes the land was treated as freehold land. Only a minuscule rent was paid to Māori, and Māori had no effective ownership.

Years later these leases of land that had been confiscated after the land wars was one of the issues I would have to resolve when I was prime minister. We needed to find an entirely different approach so that at some reasonable point, if not immediately, Māori could see a possibility of reacquiring their land, a parcel of which I had grown up on. This personal knowledge was helpful at that time. I could grasp the unfairness of the situation, and it also made me think of my early encounters with Māori as a boy.

I started out at Rahotu School, which had five teachers. It was three miles from our farm, and because this was during the early years of the war there was no school bus. Bob Horo, a Māori neighbour who farmed nearby, would drive us to school in his big family car. The large Horo family had twin boys, Sam and Murray, who were a little older than me and we were close friends during this period. And that's how I got to school and that was also my first interaction with the Māori community, which clearly was a positive one. Resting in my memory is a sad story told to me a little later by a young Māori girl who said, 'The missionaries came and taught us Māori to kneel, close our hands and eyes and look up to God, and then the Pākehā stole our land from under our feet.' A very sad story that this young girl had no doubt heard her parents tell and it's stayed in my memory for the last 75 years.

No doubt my early interaction with our Māori neighbours, at school and playing sport, helped shape my positive views regarding Māori and Māori concerns later in my political life. Also, getting to know more of Ireland's history as the years passed enabled me to see the similarities between that history and what the colonial authorities did in early New Zealand regarding land confiscations and the marginalisation of the original people.

I was always active on the farm, and from early on I understood animals. I not only understood them but I recognised them as well. When we sold the farm in 1965 we had a herd of around 120 animals, and I could trace them back to the original animals that had been on the farm 24 years earlier, just from my memory. I knew the cow that every calf was born to and so forth. I'd worked very closely with them, after all, even as a young boy, when I'd go out and check the cows at calving to see that all was well. I guess you could say animals were my thing.

Our neighbour on one side, a World War I veteran, was Victor William Henry Dawson, known as Vic. He had a slightly larger farm and herd of 40-odd cows. Mrs Dawson was a teacher at Rahotu School. The Dawsons had two children: a daughter, who was teaching at remote Whangamomona, and a son, John, who in the last year of the war joined up to train as a pilot for the air force. He never got overseas

Jim receives a word of advice from Dame Whina Cooper near the end of the unsuccessful 1987 election campaign.

— the war fortunately ended before he did — but while he was away training Vic Dawson needed help on the farm, so my parents agreed that I could stay with the Dawsons and help Vic milk his cows. I was nine years old then. I stayed there for quite a while.

Looking back, I can see this was unusual. But I was always a bit ahead of doing things. I look at nine-year-olds today, and I sure as hell wouldn't let them run the lawn, much less run a farm, but there you go. Different era, different personality.

At the Dawsons', I brought the cows into the milking shed and then helped milk and clean up afterwards, and then I went to school. I'd come home from school, get changed, help milk the cows and clean up, and go to bed. That was the routine. Vic Dawson and a couple of World War I mates always used to go fishing in March, and so when March came around I was on my own. I was 'the manager'. Another neighbour, who had been invalided home from the war and who lived two miles away, came and helped me milk the cows. As a nine-year-old, almost 10-year-old, I effectively ran that farm. I knew where the cows went and when the paddocks changed. I did all that stuff.

This was to be the start of me helping a number of neighbours with their milking, in shed after shed, herd after herd. In my last year at high school, when I was 15, I was away from home staying with people, friends of my parents, who were much further away from our farm than Vic Dawson. That farmer, Joe Brophy, was an earlier Irish immigrant and another World War I veteran. Like so many others, Joe didn't talk about the horrors of that war except once. He told me that when he was fighting in the trenches in France he was always 'first to go over the top' when it was time to advance, except for once when his mate tapped him on the back when he was about to go and said something like 'For luck, this time I'll go first'. He did, and he was cut in half by machine-gun fire as he emerged. As Joe told me this there was a long pause before he added, 'That's why I am here.' He never raised the subject of the war again, and I have no doubt that the memories were too terrible.

None of this was paid work. It was all voluntary. That's how society worked at that time, I suppose. You helped others out. And I seemed to be the family member who offered the hand. Or rather, perhaps, I was always offered to give a hand.

When I was working at the Brophys' farm I would travel to Opunake District High School on the Road Services bus that went from New Plymouth to Opunake twice daily. To be picked up I had to walk a short distance to where a few other high school pupils would gather to wait for the bus. The pick-up spot was opposite the point where Lower Parihaka Road intersected with the main coast road. Most mornings while we were waiting for the bus three young children would walk up Parihaka Road on the way to nearby Pungarehu School. One of the two girls had very bright red hair — you couldn't miss it. Those three children were Peter, Joan and Ngaire Riddell and, as history records, I married that red-haired girl, Joan, in 1963 in the Pungarehu Catholic church. It was the best decision I ever made: Joan has provided loving and practical support at every step of the way of our rather complex and varied life together.

I left school early, aged 15, which was pretty standard for the time. There was no big family discussion about whether Jim would or wouldn't leave school. Probably what triggered it was that my parents had just bought another 99 acres of relatively undeveloped land and this new property needed a lot of work. During the 1930s Depression, the government had brought in various schemes to provide work for unemployed men. One such scheme was to help farmers drain their land; often the work achieved little, but the official view was that people should be doing *something* rather than nothing. In the case of this farm, people had tried to drain the land but it had failed as there was a tough pan under the topsoil, and digging by hand meant that the drains weren't deep enough to do any good so much of the land was semi-swamp. The land clearly wasn't attractive and this had kept the price down. From memory, my parents were able to buy it for under £1000. They had to borrow the money.

I grew up in a Depression-scarred society. A lot of people were fearful of another depression. The Dawsons, for instance, had owned a big American box of a car that didn't get taken out of the garage for three years, simply because they couldn't afford the petrol. When we talk about poverty today, we're really talking about it in an entirely different context.

Although I left school early I was a great book reader in the little bit of time I had between milking cows and going to bed. My parents read enthusiastically, if that's the word, mainly books from the little local library and obviously the daily newspaper. Our household took a keen interest in local political issues and, where possible, what was happening across the world. I still love reading and it's a trait that's gone on down the generations of the family. One of our granddaughters, who's only seven years old, has a reading age of about 12.

Books with lawyers in them always interested me, which has a certain irony, given that I ended up writing laws in my later life. If I'd gone to university I would have done law, I suppose, but it was a different time, and almost nobody went to university back then. This was the era before higher education became a majority pursuit. I've never felt deprived on the education front but more than once I've realised that I would have gained this or that from a longer period in formal education, and I don't have any ego when it comes to admitting that. But it didn't happen and I've educated myself through observation, listening and reading. As a result I can go and speak to a large conference or address the United Nations or whatever, with total confidence that what I'll be saying will have relevance. Perhaps I was fortunate that I had a reasonably good idea of what was relevant and what was bullshit, and I never had any enthusiasm for the latter.

Would I have gone into politics if I'd had a law degree? I don't spend much time on what might have been and besides, as you pointed out, I also ended up as a long-term chancellor at the University of Waikato. It's a role I've enjoyed. The university spent about two years recruiting me — and there's an interesting little back story to that. The then vice chancellor, Roy Crawford, who was a graduate of Queen's University, Belfast, and some members of the university council, had been trying to recruit me to the chancellor's position but I was deeply involved in many other boards and I couldn't see how I could fit it in with my other work.

Some time later, when Helen Clark was prime minister, Roy and I ended up at the same table at a state luncheon in the Beehive. I said, 'Roy, I'm sorry I couldn't take up your offer. It's not that I wasn't interested, but I just couldn't fit it in.' And he said, 'Oh, so you're interested now. Maybe we should have another chat.' That chat happened and I was persuaded to accept the position, on the grounds that Roy could keep the workload down. That didn't happen, and in fact the workload was quite heavy, but I found the engagement with the university sector very interesting.

The world of academe is intriguing and stimulating, but sometimes disappointing as well. There are an extraordinary number of bright and able people in universities. Yet the majority do not seem to have the inclination to share that knowledge other than with their students. They rely on their students to take that knowledge out to a wider community. I've urged them to be more forthcoming about this and to find ways of doing it, but I've had rather limited success. My judgement, and it's only my judgement, is that it's not a space they feel comfortable in. The odd one does, and there are the few who share their specialist knowledge in the media, but there could be many more out helping to keep the wider community better informed on issues, for example, to do with the implications of artificial intelligence on the world of work, and how we might adjust to this new world.

But let's end that education digression there. In my early years a lot was happening in wider society. Experimentation with drugs, looser sexuality, changing music trends were all things I was certainly aware of (how could anyone not have been?) but still, it was removed from my personal experience. I came from a totally abstemious home: no drugs, no alcohol. My father would have a beer in the hay paddock now and then, but that's all. My mother didn't drink at all. Joan's parents were the same. Her father was a complete teetotaller and her mother might have a glass of wine at a wedding, but that was all.

At that stage the social environment in the countryside was very different. In the winter months there were no cows to milk, and so farm lads like me would have a bit of time on their hands to play rugby and go to dances in community halls all around the mountain in Taranaki. There were these three-piece bands that toured around playing at them all. I imagine an awful lot of partnerships were formed over those years at those dances and in the Young Farmers and Country Girls clubs.

Only a small handful of young people moved far away from their communities back then. My two sisters went away to train for nursing, but a lot of young women stayed in the district and worked in the local post office or retail sector or whatever. Or they trained to become teachers, which was another destination for a lot of young women from rural communities, which is exactly what Joan did.

In saying all this I'm trying to give you a feel of what it was, that community at Rahotu. It was focused around the dairy factory, a couple of stores, a little post office, and the pub on the corner — and hard work. And that was basically that.

My parents, as I've said, had a keen interest in politics. My mother, in particular, used to listen to Parliament on 2YA (which is what National Radio was then) although my father couldn't when he was out on the farm because there weren't portable radios then. The radio was in the kitchen and she told me once that she knew the voice of every member in Parliament.

Family discussions about politics were normal and we always listened to the news. I remember my mother saying later in life that she thought at one stage that she had produced a pacifist son, because when I was about five I used to say to her, 'I wish the war was over.' She discovered that the reason for this was because my father was always going, '*Shhhhhh*! I want to hear the war news!'

Today's generation doesn't have, and can't have, a real sense of living in New Zealand when the war dominated everything. Everybody had either friends or relatives who were away at the war, some of whom would never come back. And they wanted to hear the news, because that was their only sense of connection with what was happening. And war created political debate: When are our boys coming home? Why is this the second time this has happened in just 20 years? That sort of thing. Today there's a big emphasis on the mental harm people in that situation suffer, but in that era it was almost totally ignored. You were supposed to come back and put it all behind you, pick up your shovel or your pen and carry on. We've become a little more humane now.

In addition to that, there was the political issue of the Depression. It had bankrupted many people and it also instilled the widespread fear that it could happen again. For that reason my parents would have supported the creation of the welfare state in a generic sense, but they would also have supported it because my mother, in particular, had a strong social conscience. They believed that people had to be treated fairly and they had to have an income. Mine was not a hard-line conservative family home. Remember, we're talking about Irish Catholic immigrants who knew all about a society where the gentry were often indifferent to the needs of the desperately poor.

We lived in what was then the Egmont electorate and it voted National *to the core*. I think my mother voted Labour. I remember her telling me that she had asked Mr McHardy who she should vote for in the first election held after she had arrived in New Zealand and he told her it should be the Reform Party, which is what the conservative party of the day was known as until 1936, when the Conservative and Liberal parties came together to form the National Party. But she voted Labour and Michael Joseph Savage in 1935. She mentioned more than once how Savage had given every family a £5 bonus, and the house got electricity.

My father probably would have been more likely to vote National. I don't think I ever asked him but I did go with him to a few political meetings at election time to listen to the candidates. They were of the generation that didn't talk about how they cast their votes.

After Joan and I were married in 1963 I had started to consider a change from dairy farming, which had been the only life I had known since I was a young boy, and I decided that I didn't want to be milking cows all my life. So I decided to check out sheep farming. There were a handful of sheep farms in the district but I'd never been on one. By the end of 1964 I had started looking at a few sheep farms that were for sale from the King Country to North Auckland. We found a farm on the coast north of Dargaville that we liked and could afford with the help of a vendor second mortgage. The vendor had flown down to Taranaki to, as it were, check us out and all seemed settled. So we sold our farm to a neighbour and prepared to move to Northland. Joan's parents weren't very happy that we were moving so far away. But it never happened as the vendor was somehow able to withdraw his farm from the market and so we were left landless with a herd of cows. The search for a farm was back on, and a while later we bought our current farm on the outskirts of Te Kuiti.

My political activity had begun first in the Young Farmers Club, where I assumed leadership positions and was a leading debater. Then when I was running my own farm in the King Country, I joined Federated Farmers and my engagement stepped up quite a few notches. Federated Farmers is a rural advocacy group, of course, and at the time, in the 1960s and early 1970s, there was a lot to advocate about. There were terrible industrial problems in the meat industry: strikes, endless strikes, by the freezing workers mainly. It was devastating to farmers but also devastating to stock. Total cruelty. Stock would be sent to Auckland, Waikato, Taranaki or wherever from our part of the world and then there would be a strike and the stock would stay there two or three days and then be trucked home again because the freezing workers weren't working — it was total cruelty.

I felt that the politicians of the day weren't doing anything to rectify or resolve the situation, and I and others thought the farming leadership wasn't doing enough, either. So a group of us in Te Kuiti — some from a wider area, but based out of Te Kuiti — formed a self-appointed Farmers' Action Committee in mid-1971. I missed one of the earlier meetings at which they appointed me spokesman. I was always given these jobs. I didn't campaign for them.

What we wanted to do was confront the wider community, and not least the political masters in Wellington, with the reality of the terrible conditions. There was a lot to publicise. We had severe, repetitive droughts and we had farms with little or no food for the stock. We had farms where the stock was starving. We decided to invite the politicians to come to the King Country and that we would take them around the community with us, to meet farm groups throughout the region and also address a few public meetings. We were hopeful that the upfront exposure to the disastrous conditions would persuade them to take some steps to rectify what was clearly a broken industrial relations system.

The first of those meetings was held in the old Te Kuiti civic hall. About 400 people turned up. Television cameras were there. The unfortunate spokesman for the then National government was Daniel J. Riddiford, who was minister of justice and an associate minister of labour. I gave a speech on behalf of the frustrated farmers and the broader township — we were all suffering together — which was probably powerful and brutal. Riddiford, frankly, didn't have the capacity to respond in a manner that satisfied anybody. That day in Te Kuiti was the beginning of a number of meetings.

We ended up bringing everybody, including Norman Kirk, who was then leader of the Labour Opposition. Kirk was a powerful orator. As he started speaking in a full hall in Taumarunui I surmised that he likely had less than 20 per cent support, but by the time he finished the percentage was much higher. When Rob Muldoon, who was then minister of finance, came to start his tour through the district from Te Kuiti, I was designated to travel in the car with him. We hadn't got far down Te Kuiti's short main street before, in his normal combative style, he was being critical of farmers. It didn't faze me. As I later said to some of the local team, I'd played most of my rugby in the front row and was used to close-quarter combat. In fact that somewhat robust first meeting served me well when I went into Parliament because Rob had worked out he couldn't intimidate me as he did many others. As a general rule I worked well with Rob but that didn't mean we always agreed.

I disagreed with Rob, for instance, when he brought his very generous proposals to reform national superannuation to caucus before the 1975 election. Muldoon's proposal was to pay 80 per cent of the 'average ordinary-time wage' at the age of 60. My concerns about the affordability of this were brushed aside. That didn't mean they were wrong, and in the lead-up to the 1990 election, when I was leader of the National Party, we campaigned that we would lift the age of entitlement from 60 to 65 years and the pension would be set at 65 per cent of the average ordinary-time wage. By the time we changed the law the pension had been allowed, through not adjusting it for inflation, to drop down to near that level. And now some leader has to have the courage to lift the age of entitlement again. We should celebrate the fact that we're all living longer.

Let me return to the troubled industrial climate of the early 1970s. We also took union leaders through the King Country so that they were exposed to some of the raw anger and frustration that many felt towards the antics of the Auckland Freezing Workers Union. One union leader proudly stated straight away that he was from the communist side of the union, which was not a clever thing to do given

right Jim when he first entered Parliament in 1972.

below On the farm with contractor Mick Kearins, son Stephen and daughter-in-law Toni in 2004.

there was no support for communist propaganda at that gathering.

That initial meeting in Te Kuiti, where Daniel Riddiford spoke, was the first time I had been on national television and it gave me something of a wider profile. Weeks later, when the action committee's campaign was over, I was invited to meet a broadly representative group from the National Party who, as they put it, had decided that I was the best person to take the message we'd been setting out to Wellington. They asked whether I would consider seeking the National Party nomination for the November election and stand for Parliament. I was aware that there was talk going around about getting Jim Bolger to stand for Parliament but I was very much in two minds. Joan and I had five children at this stage, I wasn't actively engaged in party politics and it was about the last thing I was thinking of doing. For the sake of completeness, I should mention that both the Labour Party and the Social Credit Party had tentatively approached me as well.

When Joan and I discussed the suggestion she said, 'If you think you can do some good there, I suppose you should go.' Or words to that effect. So I agreed to stand. There were six others running for the nomination, but from memory I won on the first ballot, and I was elected as the MP for the new King Country electorate in the 1972 election. For all of us, me, Joan, and our young family, this was to usher in a dramatic change in our lives, and it had all happened very quickly.

In my new career in politics I had to become familiar with a much wider range of issues, especially after I became minister of labour in 1978. I had to get myself up to speed. Strikes and disputes dominated the headlines, but I also knew I had to move fast to become familiar with the enormous change that was coming to the labour market thanks to rapidly advancing technology. Back then, as now, there was a general reluctance to face up to inevitable change. So I welcomed the chance to discuss these issues.

'Picking Up the Chips': The Microprocessor Challenge in New Zealand

Victoria University of Wellington, 3 May 1980

It is pleasing to see that the theme of this seminar, 'Picking Up the Chips', conveys a positive note — facing the challenges posed by the revolution in technology and developing the use of microprocessors for the benefit of society.

Although much concern is expressed on possible job loss associated with technology, it does seem to me that seminars and conferences on 'the new technology' may well become one of the great growth industries of the 1980s . . . It's as though we've all suddenly woken up and found this new force permeating and changing our community, offices and factories and we want to do something about it . . .

That revolution isn't something that is about to happen which we could stop if we wanted to. It's happening in New Zealand. The revolution has started here already. We need to examine what this technology is capable of introducing to the benefit of society, work through its implications and, above all, learn to accommodate and live with the changes.

But micro-electronic technology has in fact been developing since the Second World War . . . Microprocessors have been introduced for nearly 10 years. The next stage of development after transistors when it became possible to combine several circuit elements (i.e. transistors) on one single surface, the integrated circuit was born.

The surface on which the circuit is built is the silicon chip we know all about. There has in the last few years been a steady development in which the number of transistors that can be put in integrated form on one chip has doubled yearly. As a result it has become possible to produce increasingly complicated functions as integrated circuits, culminating in the manufacture of the microprocessor. From this has been developed the one-chip microcomputer.

The potential use of microprocessors is vast. The cost of computing power is reducing markedly . . . As chips have become cheaper, they have invaded more and more industries. In most cases, this simply represents steady evolution in electronic componentry.

Chips have become reliable, cheap and powerful enough to permit electromechanical components to be replaced by electronics in almost any application. For example, telephone exchanges. Other examples of their use include machine-based industries, where the brains of numerically based machine tools are increasingly microprocessor based, so that the most advanced models are now multifunctional, and consumer electronics, where chip components are reducing the dimensions — and cost — of radio and TV sets as well as improving their performance by remote channel selection.

New industries have also been inspired. A new market for electronic toys and games was born in 1972. Thanks to the chip, toys now talk: memory chips have given them vocabularies. The first microprocessor-based office products appeared in the late 1970s. They imply a major reorganisation of the work environment, though not overnight. Meantime, the innovations include intelligent typewriters that store and edit text; word processor systems which communicate with visual display units; intelligent telephones that store messages and telephone numbers; microprocessor-based copiers that store coded messages.

In the computer field, the microprocessor has had the biggest impact, with computerised control of factory plants and processes, based on a network of small computers located close to line operations. Rapidly falling hardware costs are another result . . .

In the early 1980s we will have the technical ability to put a computer as an information machine into every school. My colleague the minister of education is already looking at that development. Costs and benefits must be taken into account here as elsewhere.

By the mid to late 1980s, up to 75 per cent of our homes might have microcomputers . . . Already in New Zealand there are people who live at least 200 miles away from work, who never leave their homes, and work on nothing but a computer terminal. One can foreshadow the possibility that in a few years many people will spend 70 per cent of their working time at home, with small computers linked into a central system. The remainder of their time will be spent coming into work for the sort of group activities — discussing, learning new development, exploration of ideas — that are necessary to balance out working life.

Already it is possible to have access to huge amounts of information and knowledge, by pressing the controls which throw up the information on a screen, and in one's own home. Such changes foreshadow massive economic and social change within this country. Geographical disadvantages of the past will be less important as information and hence job opportunities move outwards rather than people having to move to the centre, as has happened in industrial societies for the past 200 years . . .

There can be no doubt that the change in some areas will be drastic. But change is not a new phenomenon. For example, I wonder how many of you at this seminar have digital watches? The Swiss watch industry lost 17 companies and 70,000 jobs when digital watches took off. That clearly wasn't a reason not to develop digital watches. What it suggests is that the traditional Swiss watch industry didn't respond quickly or positively enough to the change.

That is another message we must all absorb, namely, that we must respond quickly and positively. Because, as Alvin Toffler predicted in his book *Future Shock* back in 1970, innovation (such as the digital watch) will continue to grow exponentially. There is no hope, he said, of trying to stop this 'great growling engine of change' . . .

While it is simple to quantify job losses in certain areas, due to technology, it is more difficult to assess job losses resultant upon the continuation of outdated techniques and a loss of market competitiveness. But unquestionably without change huge job losses will occur for these reasons.

At this stage it is possible to identify three possible strategies that New Zealand might adopt in response to the impact of technological change. There is what I call the control approach, in which it is argued that there should be a mechanism to control the rate of introduction of technology and suggests that criteria should be established for new equipment which match national priorities and have union and industry agreement. This implies an elaborate and slow procedure which would lead to slower investment and, I believe, slower economic growth and loss of international competitiveness. It also implies a capacity for detailed planning in this area, which I don't believe exists.

Then there is the *laissez faire* approach, which will allow market forces alone to determine the rate of introduction of technology and to determine the response of the labour market. Such an approach would imply a lack of interest by government in the impact of technology on the labour market, which is incorrect.

The approach I prefer is one that contains an element of compromise. It would seek to minimise the adverse effects of technology change by positive action, rather than negative controls. It would foster employment growth and ease the adaptions necessary in the labour market by helping those individuals adversely affected and encourage new attitudes towards necessary adjustments during working life. It would also require the active promotion of innovation by encouraging investment and developing employer awareness of opportunity presented by modern technology.

This approach is the most appealing, given that the primary objective of policy is to encourage the productive investment needed to maintain international competitiveness. Employment levels can only be maintained or increased in the long term through the growth of efficient sectors of the economy. This policy could, however, be frustrated by lack of enterprise by employers and/or uncooperative attitudes by employees because of fears of the adverse effects of new technology. The option I am suggesting endeavours to see that this does not occur.

New Zealand, I believe, is particularly well suited to beneficially incorporate micro-electronics in our industry because of the short and varied production runs which are common here. We also have a low population density but a large resource base with the potential in areas such as energy only now being realised. What we need now is a flowering of Kiwi ingenuity, so that we devise new uses for technology first, such as the recently developed computer-controlled petrol pump.

In this area we can't simply borrow blueprints from overseas and neither can central government be expected to provide all the answers. The private sector must be active in seeking out new business opportunities that will provide jobs for the New Zealand workforce.

Along with this it is necessary that management, when planning to introduce new technology, gets alongside its workforce as early as possible, to discuss change and all its ramifications. How many jobs will be replaced and how quickly? How many people will require new training or re-employment in other areas of work? . . .

In the retraining area, additional work is required to determine the precise responsibilities of employers and government . . . I personally do not see retraining and skill upgrading being the sole responsibility of the taxpayer. Those in the education field are already grappling with the challenge of what type of education young New Zealanders should receive, so as to equip them for the world of tomorrow . . .

I believe the microcomputer is among the most important tools in a modern society. The only question is, have we the will to use it along with our other advantages to lift New Zealand onto a new plane of development? Can we build on it positively with a sense of national urgency? It can provide new strategic opportunities in our industries, in our trade, and in our resource development . . .

While experts know with precision how a chip is made and can predict with some certainty future development, no one can predict with absolute precision the impact of new technology on society. But the strength of man is not the precision by which he reacts to certain development but his capacity to adapt to new circumstances.

It will be a measure of our maturity as a nation how we react to the exciting new frontiers that 'picking up the chips' will entail.

The Altar

Jim is laughing, but with an element of self-deprecation, as we swerve off the conversational path one morning in the company of his wife, Joan, who still speaks with something of a teacher's note of authority.

These two have been married for longer than most New Zealanders have been alive. They have nine children. Kids are an issue Jim returns to elsewhere, in, for instance, his views on low fertility rates in the Western world. He says he is optimistic about the current younger generation 'for which I have great expectations'.

This morning is less about expectations than reflections, however, as we're talking about the couple's own relationship. It has always been something of an anomaly that people in my line of media work can become excited about a prime minister parenting one child, while others with much larger families (not just Jim but later Bill English as well) don't rate a journalistic mention. And nor is it just because these are men: Jim's first finance minister, Ruth Richardson, nursed a daughter in Parliament and much of the reporting of this was not gushing.

Perhaps it's just the era. Jim and Joan met in 1960, after all, when Jim was young and politically undistinguished, in an old world now lost to the contemporary solar system. When television was just beginning and long before the ceaseless, if highly uncertain, charms of social media. And still being together after all this time is perhaps not the contemporary political style, either. How well suited they still are, and how nice to have a change from our usual one-on-one format to talk about things marital and extramarital. We start with the subject of children.

Jim: Our oldest and youngest kids are about 17 years or so apart in age — they stretched out a little further towards the end . . .

Joan: That gap was quite good, because when those three youngest ones came along, there were lots of older ones to help out. We had C = critical mass. But you have to wait a while to get that.

Jim: We had supportive parents to help Joan. My mother was widowed before our first child was born. My father died of cancer in 1962, 10 years before I got into politics. He was just 64. He was a smoker but it was actually cancer of the stomach, not the lungs, that killed him. I won't pretend I know why.

My mother was always willing to come to us, and her family was her life. And what a life. She ended up with 27 grandchildren. She would always go to whoever was having the next baby and help out. She was an extraordinary, strong woman with a fantastic work ethic. She died at 104. Good genes. You might have to put up with me for a long time. In fact, with modern medicine, I might even live longer.

Joan's teaching background was more than helpful in bringing up this large group of young people and all the education input that's needed to do that. Joan's parents were also always ready to help where possible, as they did in 1977 when I was on that overseas trip as minister of fisheries. It was a cultural thing, too. There was this simple commitment from our parents that their grandchildren would be looked after. Having nine children was never a burden to Joan and me. I know others might look at the size of the family and think so, but really, no, not at all.

Joan: And generally we escaped the media attention when it came to the children.

Jim: Even though ours was quite notable in being larger than most, everybody in politics has had a family. Joan and I grew up in the same community. When we first met, our families were known to each other. And, as I've said, when I was doing that milking for the Brophys in my last year of high school I used to catch the school bus opposite the beach side of Lower Parihaka Road, where Joan's parents had a small farm. I would see these three young people — Joan's brother, her younger sister, and Joan — go around that corner many times. A bright red-headed girl going around to Pungarehu School, which was just walking distance from their farm . . . I knew who this young redhead was for a long time. But the way we actually met, was through Young Farmers Club, which I was active in, and Country Girls Club.

I was the lead debater in our Young Farmers Club, which had a history of having a strong debating team at that time. Debating was also an important part of the club's social life, which is why some young women from Rahotu who were at the teachers' training college in Palmerston North came to watch the Rahotu team in the North Island debating final being held in Palmerston North. We won.

above The Bolger family photographed the morning after the 1990 election victory. From left: Matthew, Paul, Aidan, Bernadette, Joan, Fiona, Rachael, Jim holding grandson Sam, Dan, Brian, daughter-in-law Toni holding Jacinta, Stephen.

left Jim and Joan photographed at Premier House in 1991.

Afterwards, the girls came up and Joan said to me out of the blue, 'You should have been a priest.'

Joan: Actually, he should've been.

Jim: I obviously had an authoritative style, thank you. [*laughs*] But clearly, she gave very little help for me becoming a priest.

Joan: And you coached our debating team.

Jim: That's right. I coached the Rahotu Country Girls debating team, which was Joan, Lois Butler, another local girl who was at training college with Joan, and Anna Kuriger, who my younger brother married a few years later. And that part of the family is now represented in Parliament: Barbara Kuriger was elected the National MP for the Taranaki–King Country electorate in 2014.

Joan: The dances that were held all along the Taranaki coast and around Mount Taranaki by Young Farmers Clubs were a big social thing. We didn't go to bars as people do nowadays. Those dances were the social glue in rural areas.

Jim: It was a different environment and the social structures were different. All the families were bigger. Many of the girls went away and became teachers or nurses. The lads did something else. And people did tend to get married younger. They didn't live together before marriage. That would have been severely frowned upon.

Joan: Oh, very frowned upon. Yes. It was a different social climate altogether.

Jim: The society we're in now — and this is true across the world — is more liberal. It's more acceptable to do things that were totally unacceptable in our youth. That, I guess, has just been an evolution in the 57 years we've been married and the 60-odd years since we first started going out. That's how it is. I don't really pass judgement. I don't know if it's going backwards or forwards since we married in 1963 in the church in Pungarehu.

The question sometimes comes up about pressure on the marriages of politicians. And there's no question there are pressures. Joan and I were talking about this while we were out walking this morning, and we were remembering that I missed a lot of the children's events — whether it was a school presentation or playing sport or a birthday. I simply couldn't be there because I was in some other part of the country or back in my electorate. The first three years were the hardest because I was a backbencher and Joan was at home on the farm with the children while I was in Wellington for the working week. You couldn't get home on Thursday night. You came down to Wellington on the Tuesday, and you left on the Friday, late.

Back then MPs had to look after a massive electorate in between times. The local Ōtaki electorate where we now live here on the Kapiti Coast has four National Party branches. When I was told that recently I thought they sounded proud about it. But in my electorate, King Country, we had 33 branches, many in remote back-country venues. The workload was quite heavy as we didn't have professional staff allocated to the electorate in those early years.

Joan: People would ring me. Then they'd be shocked when Jim wasn't there because he was in Wellington . . .

Jim: 'What's he doing? What's he doing in Wellington?' they'd say.

It required great tolerance on Joan's behalf. But that was the life that had been chosen. And that we all got through is a great credit to Joan and the family.

You ask how does a man in these positions deal with the pressure to have affairs? I think it's personal values. Well, for me it is. I have seen reports that the American vice president, Mike Pence, won't go into a room alone with a woman other than his wife, but I never had rules like that. I was totally capable of managing myself if there [*laughs*] was someone else in the room, if you want to put it that way, and so can most people. We tend to focus on the ones who don't, but the great majority do manage themselves as far as that goes.

Joan: It's your own values, certainly.

Jim: I've said this at I don't know how many graduation ceremonies at the university: You must live your values. And for me, for us, it's the same, and adultery is not one of those values. I'm not certain that the education system — I have this discussion with universities — teaches values or ethics sufficiently. It's great to teach young people how to run a computer or write lucidly, but in order to live a balanced life, you have to have values. Which, yes, brings up the question of whether teachers should be doing it or whether . . .

Joan: It should come from the home really.

Jim: I was talking to Matthew, our son, about this recently. He went to Georgetown University in Washington, which isn't far from the New Zealand embassy when we were there. It was a Jesuit college originally — back in the late 1700s it became the first Catholic university in the United States — but I don't know if there are any priests there now.

He did international business as his core degree but they also taught ethics. I remember Matthew talking about what it covered: respect for other people, their cultures, creeds and religious beliefs.

Joan: It was useful. They had to go out and teach in underprivileged schools. They went to schools on the Mexican border to see a different side of life.

Jim: But of course the subject is always evolving. Today we have sexual issues that simply wouldn't have been discussed in my youth. And then there's the fact that there isn't a clear-cut consensus but at least two major perspectives: the very hardline one that Israel Folau and others like him espouse, that gay people are all doomed to hell. And the more accommodating view that a percentage of society is born with — I don't know what the right word is — the predisposition to find far more comfort and companionship with someone of the same sex rather than the other way around.

And then, going back to the morals question, there's the church teaching, too. I would think that helps marriages stay together, but then you also have a majority of marriages that stay together in which the couples don't go to church every week. In our case, though, it's our belief structure and I'm comfortable with it. I've never found it difficult. On most occasions, if I'm overseas in some strange and distant country, I will find out where the church is and attend mass there. Lives that, like ours, have a strong Christian base have one set of values. Those who grow up with a different belief system obviously base their lives on those teachings. I don't find it difficult that others see things slightly differently or dramatically differently. I'm not out there to convert the world to my views on that at all. This is just me. This is just us.

Church

Among the framed photographs that enjoy pride of place in the small gallery of portraits hanging in the Bolger home is one showing Jim and Karol Wojtyła, better known to millions as Pope John Paul II. The two — actually three, because an obviously impressed Joan is in the photograph, too — met at the Vatican and elsewhere, including in New Zealand, during Jim's ministerial years. It was an encounter between two leaders, but of course it was also one of a church member meeting his spiritual leader. Or should that be ideological leader? Jim's Catholicism, after all, is his philosophy — but, as he cautions, that word needs to be used lightly.

Still, Catholic leaders haven't exactly been a dime a dozen in most historically Protestant nations. In both Britain and the United States, countries that have had precisely one such elected leader between them over the period of their combined histories, there has been outright prejudice based on a perception that Catholic premiers are influenced by the Vatican on matters such as abortion rights. Yet, as Jim points out, a little wearily at one stage, the same issue doesn't seem to arise when discussing leaders from other faith backgrounds or those who might have been, for instance, Freemasons. On a brighter note, New Zealand has also had a number of Catholic prime ministers, including the much-revered Michael Joseph Savage and Joseph Ward.

On the road and off, for all his life, the experience of the Eucharist has always been an important part of Jim's weekly ritual. Such was the case in the immediate aftermath of the 15 March 2019 Christchurch massacre, when he was at the Nizami Ganjavi International Center conference in Baku, the capital of mainly Muslim Azerbaijan. The Center has many former heads of state and diplomats on its board. He was very taken by the empathetic outreach from the conference participants to him and Joan and also to former prime ministers Helen Clark and Jenny Shipley, who were also there. At Jim's request, the local organisers arranged for a driver and interpreter to ferry him and Joan to Sunday mass at the local Church of the Virgin Mary's Immaculate Conception.

The pontiff leads the world's largest church, but he is also a political leader — and a strong leader, too, in John Paul's case. When we think of strong leaders, though, we think of those who lead militarily powerful nations. That's not an option these days for the Holy See or for New Zealand. Thus, I suppose, Stalin's famous line about the Pope not being somebody to fear. How many divisions, after all, does he command?

But can power be measured only in those terms? New Zealand has little or no military muscle to speak of yet our 'independent' foreign policy has long been shorthand for a kind of soft moral barrage that causes other nations to take note and even accord us respect. Such is the conceit, at any rate, and one doesn't need to torture it too hard to see a certain religious impulse bubbling beneath the political surface.

On this particular morning, though, we were down for a more personal conversation about the church and its role in Jim's own life and times. At one point, the personal element cut two ways, when Jim alluded a little balefully to a newspaper article that had appeared early on in his political leadership examining the role Catholicism may or may not play in his leadership style. The not terribly good article had in fact been written by yours truly for the old *Evening Post* newspaper, appearing just a few days before the October 1990 election. Such embarrassments.

It has seemed through my long public life that my Catholic faith has attracted a particular amount of interest. It has always surprised me, given that it's the largest Christian denomination in the world. An example is a documentary that was put together of interviews with me and others when I became leader of the National Party. I couldn't help but notice that the documentary emphasised about three times that I was a Catholic. We're talking about the mid-1980s, and Catholicism was supposedly still a factor in the minds of a lot of people, something I don't accept at all. But if you go back 50 years to the 1930s and 1940s, it was different.

My parents didn't bring much with them to Depression-era New Zealand, but they did carry a big tradition: the Catholic faith. Not only involvement with the church itself but also the way they interacted with that interpretation of the Christian message, the belief system and the obligations that went with it. And I think *obligation* is probably the word: they saw it as an obligation as Catholics to attend mass on Sunday, but of course many don't.

The church was important to both of them and therefore to the children they raised. My parents didn't have a big circle of friends, other than their neighbours and those, as far as I can recall, they knew through church, which we went to every Sunday.

At first we used to go to church in an old four-curtain-sided Chevy, but then we got a little converted pick-up truck (which was a habit of that day: farmers and local engineers would get an old American square car and make it into a little pick-up truck) and we would go to mass on the back of the truck, come wind or rain.

The Māori–Irish links in our part of the country were interesting. The priest in our parish, an Irishman called Father Eugene Carmine, always drew analogies between the many aspects of Māori culture and Irish culture. He described Māori, in a friendly tone, as 'brown-skinned Irishmen' — which was to say, he saw a shared spiritual dimension.

Mind you, there were a lot of Catholics in coastal Taranaki to begin with. Just like the West Coast of the South Island, that part of the North Island had a lot of Irish immigrants. It was reinforced, after World War II, by a lot of Dutch migrants; many of them were Catholic also. That said, the community was not a microcosm of Ireland, but a lot of us had Irish links — as did most of the priests in that era. Even so, there was no convent school nearby so we went to the local state school with all our neighbours, which is why I've always said that all my mistakes can be blamed on the state school system, because they were the only schools I attended.

The Catholic Church, until the Second Vatican Council in the early 1960s, was a conservative structure reflecting the views and attitudes of earlier centuries. But Vatican II, which involved all the bishops of the church and large numbers of the laity — and in a gesture of outreach to other Christian denominations there were many observers from other churches in attendance — sought to move it forward. The council held four sessions between 1962 and

1965. It was a massive exercise and brought about many changes in church ritual; for example, moving away from the Latin language to the language of the country where the mass was being celebrated, and very much more in terms of how the mass was organised, but not the central belief of the eucharist. Of course there were conservative members of the church who disagreed.

The 16 documents that came out of those deliberations also changed the relationship of the Catholic Church with other churches, because it now no longer saw itself as the sole vehicle through which you could have redemption. What happened with that transformation was hugely important to the development of the community not only in New Zealand but also around the world.

Personally, I think the evolution was totally logical. Changing from Latin to the local language — well, why wouldn't you? Or maybe that's what I thought because I didn't have any Latin, hadn't been to a convent school and was taught my catechism after mass by some well-meaning (and good) ladies. To me, praying in a language one doesn't understand makes no sense, even if I could see that it was about the centrality of Rome — something that had already been challenged with the Reformation. Although we should remember, as well, that the English part of the Reformation was driven in part by the desire of King Henry VIII to have another wife, rather than for any deep religious reason. Henry had six wives: two he divorced, two he had beheaded, one died after childbirth and one outlived him. From my perspective, the much more substantive challenge to the church practice and rituals of the time was the challenge Martin Luther levelled at the church and its papal authority. I'll leave it there as I don't pretend to be a theologian.

If you jump all those centuries from there to where we are now, the church is desperately trying to address a particular subject that

Among Jim's more personally notable encounters was the one he and Joan enjoyed with the reform-minded Pope John Paul II.

has been hidden from the public eye for a long time: sexual abuse. It's essential that this is eradicated. The hiding of that abuse has been an *incredible* mistake, or, in the terminology of the church, an incredible sin. I welcome the fact that the church is moving to deal with this. But it's not only the Catholic Church that has been caught up with sexual abuse claims. Such abuse is also across society, including other churches. It's an issue that we all have to address.

The celibacy of priests — and indeed the fact that only men are priests — is still deeply embedded in the past. But being embedded in the past isn't always wrong. Some people might look at Māori and other indigenous cultures as being embedded in the past. They might ask, 'Why don't they come up to date?' The Catholic Church is in that same space. People ask the same thing.

But what's embedded in the past for centuries is difficult to change. Understandably so, at one level. I recall one of the treaty settlements I was involved with many years later in politics — I don't think I'll name the person. This senior Māori leader withdrew, emotionally and in tears, before he agreed to the settlement in my office, because he wondered whether he had the authority. After all, this had been a grievance that his forebears could find no answer to. How did he have the authority to sign off on one? I think, albeit in a different way, the church is in that place. Pope Francis, I'm sure, wants a solution, but finding the correct way forward is a challenge in a community of over a billion people — but I'm confident the correct way forward will be found.

I mean, nobody suggests the early Apostles were always celibate. In fact, the clergy used to be largely married men. It wasn't until about the fourth century that the leaders of the church decided that priests should be celibate. And not every branch of Christianity supports clerical celibacy. Different branches have different requirements.

I don't subscribe to the view that the only authentic voice is the one articulated by the Catholic Church. I was talking about this in a recent speech. I said I thought it would be an extraordinary and judgemental God who decided that the accident of birth would determine whether you were saved or not. In other words, you would be saved because you were born into a Catholic family. If you were unfortunate enough not to be, then bad luck. Once I started to think about it, it never resonated with me.

But then I think we've got to go wider in the world today. One of the great challenges is the religious divide in the minds of many between Islam and Christianity. You see this played out perhaps most strongly in the United States; when President Trump was elected he tried to bar immigration from majority-Muslim countries. Fortunately, the courts told him to get lost, or legal words to that effect. But if you stand back and take a holistic view, and if you believe in a just God, then you cannot believe in such a condemnation of those who by accident of birth were born into a different faith family or a different religion. It cannot be so.

I think we're going to see more change in religious practice. That'll be challenging for some. Some people do find change in all walks of life extraordinarily difficult. In fact, in my political career I have found that change is *the* most frightening word in the language. I think back to the massive protests that I faced as minister of labour when I introduced a straightforward law change to permit, not require, shops to open on Saturdays, when more people had time to shop. A later government opened shops on Sundays.

This reluctance to accept change is surprising in New Zealand, given that we are children of change. We are all descendants of those who had the courage to take the risk to go to some strange and distant land. And that history of being prepared to face the unknown is where we get our willingness to take bigger risks in, for example, social reforms, not just locally but also in response to what's happening in the wider world.

I'm the middle of my parents' five children. My oldest brother, John, who's fully retired, farmed all his life, first in coastal Taranaki, and then in the northern King Country. His wife, Marie, was also a coastal Taranaki girl. In fact, the first farm they had was quite close to where her family farmed. They had five children, but tragically lost their eldest son, Peter, in a car crash when he was a teenager. That was a terrible blow.

My eldest sister, Carmel, trained as a nurse — in fact, both of my two sisters trained as nurses at New Plymouth Public Hospital. You trained on the job in those days. From talking to others over the years who worked with them, I understand that they both were superbly good nurses in terms of their outreach to patients. After she qualified, Carmel and a couple of other nurses travelled around Australia for about two years, nursing. When she came back to New Zealand she reconnected with a South Canterbury farmer she had met when she was nursing in Timaru, and her mature life was as a sheep farmer's wife in inland South Canterbury and an employee of Statistics New Zealand for almost 30 years. Her role was to travel the highways and byways to personally interview randomly selected people to gather detailed data for the department.

Carmel is staunchly Catholic, and her husband, Alan, nearly always went to mass with her on Sundays even though he wasn't Catholic. Towards the end of his life, he told her he wished to become a Catholic, and he was received into the church. He was very comfortable with his decision, I think is the way I'd put it. Carmel was also staunchly anti-abortion; she became a leader in that campaign, and received a papal citation for her work.

My younger sister, Kathleen Bernadette, whom the family calls Bernie, did all her nursing in New Plymouth and then she met and married Pat Prendiville, an Irishman from County Kerry who had come to New Zealand a few years before. He was a builder, but he had grown up on a small farm on that rugged peninsula in the south-west region of Ireland. They later bought a farm on Kahui Road almost opposite where Joan's parents farmed. They farmed there for many years. In retirement, they went back to New Plymouth.

My brother Paddy, who was next in the family after me, worked in a dairy company for a while before going farming. Later he became a real estate agent and he has been in that business for so long that I don't think even he knows. He says he's the oldest real estate agent in New Zealand.

So yes, it was a family of farmers and nurses. Not all of us went on to have large families ourselves. Kathleen, for instance, had no children of her own, although she and Pat did adopt four children, which was a great credit to them both. Carmel had four children. Paddy also has four, and John five. Those are all quite large families by today's standards but that number was not such a big deal 50 years ago. Joan and I, with our nine children, are the outliers.

It's good we're talking about family sizes because this also touches on an issue that's happening particularly in the white world, which is to say, the family is basically dying out as fertility levels drop, which in turn has a relevance to the rise of white nationalism, with fearful, paranoid people staring out at a world changing before their eyes. So let's digress a bit. Let's look at Europe in the eighteenth and nineteenth century. Donald Trump talks about immigrant invasions and so forth, but in actual fact the real invasion, historically speaking, was out of Europe in the 1700s and 1800s, an invasion that would eventually dominate many aspects of the known world — Europe, the Americas, much of Africa, and moving into Asia. Think of India, which was considered the jewel in the crown of the British Empire — until it gained independence in 1947, which in my mind signalled the beginning of the end of the empire. A sad and at times tragic aspect of the invasion from Western Europe, and the colonisation of much of the known world, is that in most instances the colonised indigenous people were first marginalised in their own countries, then had to fight bitter battles to regain their independence.

And now it's the reverse in some ways. It's fascinating. The descendants of European expansion have apparently decided to have a smaller role in the world, as very low birthrates mean that, generation after generation, they are a diminishing force. Because there is no replacement birthrate in any white-majority country in the world (or any white group in a non-white-majority country). There's a growing fear among some white people that they are in a world that's vanishing. I really think that's what's driving this extreme white nationalistic racist theology or ideology, which itself is terribly tragic and terribly hard to combat. Because there's absolutely no sign that the world will do other than become more brown.

It's a voluntary change. White people have chosen it, they've chosen to have small families, and part of that choice is a belief by many that the world has become overpopulated, and much is *certainly* economics. Housing costs have been the driver of most of the change. When I was growing up 80 years ago — and this is true of Joan, too — we lived in very modest households. In fact, the places where Joan grew up were less than modest: they would not be used today. The house I grew up in was perfectly sound but it was small and very limited.

The world has made extraordinary progress in recent times — slashing absolute poverty rates, and so on — except when it comes to families, which are under huge pressure. Up until modern times, most households survived on the income of one breadwinner. Nowadays, that's virtually impossible. Why? Well, the biggest issue is obviously the cost of housing, and in New Zealand, for reasons I really don't understand, we can't seem to get on top of it. The current government came in on a great promise to make everything right with KiwiBuild — they were going to build this, they were going to build that — and it has been a total failure. An abject failure.

Society, then, for better or worse, has changed and is changing. The social implications of everybody having to work to survive has changed the dynamics of households, the size of families and so on. Sadly, at the moment, it's not getting better. I saw somewhere that CEO salaries have increased by 900-and-something per cent over the last while, whereas the average worker's is up by 12 per cent in real terms. So much for neoliberalism.

Let's go back a bit and consider all the migrants who came to New Zealand from the time of European settlement. We mainly welcomed people from the British Isles, unlike Australia, which after World War II also welcomed more from southern Europe as well, taking in Italians, Greeks and people from the Balkans, among others, and different religions. We were conservative. We existed in a world that didn't spend much time looking at the world that was emerging after the colonial powers were, in most cases, forced to withdraw. We didn't seem to notice that the change was starting.

This is one of the big grouches I have with how we treat our history. When I was growing up, we regarded Māori New Zealanders as brown-skinned Pākehā. We said they were clever because they'd adopted our ways and attitudes and language very quickly. We diminished their own uniqueness and their own considerable skills. We're only really starting to get on top of that now. We still have difficulty in teaching a totally honest history of New Zealand's colonial period, but I welcome the fact that it is now government policy to do this. I hope that they are successful.

New Zealand is not alone. Politicians around the world have their own problems with teaching history — and discussing the future. German Chancellor Angela Merkel got into an awful lot of trouble by allowing in a million refugees, mainly from the Middle East and North Africa. I personally thought it was a remarkable gesture, not least because of the extraordinary wisdom in it. She knows that the German people are having much smaller families and as such Germany is an ageing society. She knows, as a smart leader, the country needs all those new workers.

Yes, it has created tension, but let's look at the reason again. It has caused some tension because of centuries of dominance by white people. Some white people find it difficult to accept that others who don't look like them are going to become more dominant and will hold leading positions across the world, including across white Europe. Many have no problem in hiring different ethnicities to do work they want done, but the thought that these people would emerge as leaders is outside their comfort zone. But that is all changing: you only have to watch the international news channels and note the range of ethnicities presenting the shows and how many appear as expert commentators.

For example, the British Parliament now, like the New Zealand Parliament, has a range of ethnicities and naturally they are coming through to senior positions. It's just now starting to manifest itself at the senior levels of government and industry. None of this is surprising or out of kilter with the societies Britain and other countries have become and are becoming. What we don't seem to have been able to do — and when I say *we*, I mean the world — is prepare our societies for this inevitable change. The change is happening in the ethnic mix and the culture of countries. This is happening at the same time that the development of artificial intelligence and robotics and automation of the most sophisticated kind is challenging the traditional workplace. All these developments are totally transforming the workplace and, more broadly, societal structures. Decades back the world transitioned from a society where there was a single wage earner to one where it is normal for both partners to be in paid employment, yet despite that doubling of earning capacity, many exist from pay cheque to pay cheque. We really are in an era of change and challenge.

It has taken the Covid-19 pandemic to force society to find a new way of working. Equally challenging will be how we can develop a different approach to economics to achieve a more equitable sharing of wealth. There is something wrong when people in full-time employment in good jobs still require welfare payments to survive.

Can Politics be Christian?

Victoria University of Wellington, 10 April 1984

Thanks for inviting me to discuss the challenging issue of 'Can politics be Christian?' You did not ask the even more challenging questions of whether politics are Christian or whether they should be Christian. I suspect that underlying the question was the thought that politics is such a dog eat dog profession that it is unlikely to be Christian.

Many, I am sure, would accept the view that sees a politician as often the kind of person who would cut down a tree and then stand on the stump and give a speech about conservation.

For the purpose of this discussion let me define politics as the science of government — administering public affairs and setting up laws and regulations to govern society. No one suggests that all citizens will agree with a particular law or the general thrust of policy in given areas. Therefore, to prevent abuse or tyranny there needs to be checks on the authority and power of those practising politics.

Some seek to establish those checks by recourse to a written constitution, but in my view the most effective restraint is through free and open elections. In other words, the ballot box. It should also be said in discussing the generality of politics that political decision-making is based on obtaining either a majority or a consensus in favour of a certain course of action.

While that form of decision-making is the basis of democratic politics and is certainly sufficient to write law, it cannot be said that such procedures could ever be a final and enduring determination of what is right and wrong. Because of the ballot box mentioned earlier, changes in public opinion may mean that another group of politicians reverses or amends the earlier decision. An essential element, therefore, of politics is that decisions lack permanence, compared with the unchanging truths of Christianity.

In seeking to determine whether politics can be Christian we must determine what is demonstrably different about the Christian belief. By doing this we can seek to measure politics against a particular standard. In a pluralistic society this can be very difficult and in fact the rest of this discussion could be taken up with a search for an agreed definition of the Christian viewpoint.

Many would focus on the caring aspects of Christ's teaching as typified by the story of a man set upon by robbers and left on the roadside half dead. Many saw him and walked by. But it was the Samaritan who displayed a Christian concern and provided for his care. This story of concern for one's less fortunate brothers finds modern expression through the countless acts of many individuals and groups as well as through the development of sensitive welfare assistance.

Some might suggest that there is an element of forced Christianity because those who may not wish to be Samaritans are required to be through the workings of the tax system. However, it must be said that many who reject Christian teaching strongly support social justice through a just economic order and a humane welfare system. Atheistic communism would claim to be seeking to achieve just that. It is therefore necessary to look closely at the reasons for offering help and for developing a welfare system if we are to have a true appreciation of the Christian message.

Christians do not support such work simply because having a healthy community conforms with some economic theory. Nor is it because of some transient value placed on man by man. It is because of the intrinsic worth of each individual person. Individual worth attracts Christian love, no matter how unattractive the individual person may be.

A beautiful present-day example of this Christian love must surely be that of Mother Teresa and her care for the poorest of the poor in India. This unselfish love for each individual is, I believe, the central core of Christian teaching — the inalienable worth and dignity of each individual human person. This is not something bestowed by man. It is determined by God. It is for this reason that Mother Teresa, among others, cares in a personal way with her own hands for the destitute.

Palmerston North's Catholic Bishop, Peter Cullinane, put it another way in a small publication of his recently when he noted: 'The Gospel by itself does not offer even an outline for social or economic planning. Rather it highlights the real importance of the people whose needs must be met by social and economic planning. It does this by giving us a new basis for estimating human worth. Namely God's own unconditional and undiscriminating love for every person.'

He goes on to observe the difference this makes when, for instance, 'Specific items of social and economic planning are examined not only in the light of their financial returns or their political expediency or technical feasibility but also in the light of their compatibility with human dignity.'

He states further: 'Indeed, commitment to the paramount value of persons undergirds the conviction that economic realities and political options should be subject to ethical evaluation.'

The difficulty with translating that ideal into political reality is that on many issues, tragically, Christians are deeply divided. The great moral debate on the admissibility of abortion and euthanasia is one example. Another is whether it is in conformity with Christian teaching to own weapons of mass destruction such as nuclear arms, or whether the concept of a nuclear deterrent is an acceptable Christian response to a country's defence needs.

One of the clear difficulties therefore in determining whether politics can be Christian is that Christians are deeply divided and confused on issues that are central to the Christian message. This is not something peculiar to today's world.

It is perhaps helpful in answering the question 'Can politics be Christian?' to look at one of the great debates of earlier years in the Christian/political arena, the question of the slave trade. At the end of the eighteenth century and in the early part of the nineteenth century the slavery question divided England. Those who supported slavery argued their case on two grounds. First, that the trade was an economic necessity. Second, that no moral principle was being overturned because slaves were regarded as property, not individuals. In other words they were 'non-persons'. The question of humanity did not arise in most people's minds.

A celebrated case illustrating this point took place in 1783 after the owner of a vessel had 132 slaves thrown overboard in order to profit from the insurance. Both sides in the case ignored the loss of 132 lives. It was, the attorney-general of the time said, 'a case of goods and chattels — a throwing of goods overboard to save the residues'. The law, said the then chief justice, was 'exactly as if horses had been thrown overboard'. The solicitor-general deprecated the 'pretended appeal' to humanity and agreed the master had the unquestioned right to drown as many as he wished.

There are other examples, but this case demonstrates graphically that 200 years ago the laws of England did not reflect the intrinsic value and worth of the individual human person, if that person happened to be a slave. The slave trade debate also reminds us that large segments of Christian opinion and civil law can ignore Christian values for a long time on specific issues and yet in the end return to them. In this instance it was the reaffirmation of the human dignity of man compared with the earlier description of slaves as chattels.

It was the committed Christian parliamentarian William Wilberforce who for 20 years led the battle in the British Parliament to change the law on the slave trade, before finally getting support for abolition in 1833. Much closer to our time, in the same general area of law — the equal worth of all human persons — was the move in the United States to outlaw segregation on racial grounds. The practice of apartheid in South Africa is a constant reminder that there are still those who apparently accept Christian teaching but still deny the equal worth of all people.

There are other developments in the political world which are clearly in accord with Christian teaching. For example, Prime Minister Muldoon's campaign to establish a more just and fair trade and payment system in the world, while clearly seeking to benefit New Zealand's trading position, also reflects a wider concern that the present system is perpetuating the imbalance between those who have and those who have not.

Last year, when speaking as president of the International Labour Conference before the representatives of government, workers and employers from 150 nations, I commented on the same issue and noted that it will be necessary for those who have much to share with those who have little. Further, it is not just a matter of aid programmes, it is also a matter of sharing opportunity within and between countries through trade. On that occasion I noted that if as individuals we ignore our responsibility then nations will ignore theirs.

So in the end it comes back to us as individuals. If as individuals we are committed to Christian objectives then politics will reflect that. But, as I have shown, on various major issues the Christian community is divided on what is the true interpretation of the Christian message.

This division will also be reflected in politics. That may mean, as I have shown on the question of slavery, that the politics of an era may not reflect a Christian view. Therefore in giving a positive 'yes' to the question 'Can politics be Christian?', I note that they may not always be so. However, concluding that politics can be Christian only raises the further questions of whether they are and whether they should be. On the latter question my firm view is that they should be. Not in the sense of seeking to incorporate a particular denominational view in civil law, but with the purpose of providing a constant base for the civil law. Without moral absolutes as a cornerstone, the world becomes a much less secure place for individuals.

The point is, if our only criterion for judging ethical action is the current collective conscience, then we have no fixed standard whatever. Simple collective conscience constantly alters, with the result that an individual's protection is not through unchanging moral values but through public mood in the marketplace. There is little doubt that the major reason for the great upsurge in the number of abortions is due to a denial of the long-held Christian absolute of the unique and intrinsic value of each individual.

Already the momentum is gathering to deny also the unique worth of each of us as we move towards old age. Demographic projections show graphically that in New Zealand, as in other Western countries, there is a rapidly ageing population. The percentage of old and dependent persons, as against those engaged in productive work, is increasing yearly. I am sure you require no prompting to see the dilemma — or is it the mortal peril? — you and I will face if the politicians of tomorrow seek the same solution for an ageing population as this generation has accepted to control population growth.

There are no economic arguments to justify maintaining a large, ageing population. Already some people in authority are making ominous comments. In the *Dominion* of March 30th it was reported that Governor Richard Lamm of Colorado suggested that terminally ill old people have 'a duty to die and get out of the way'.

While there are no economic arguments to sustain the aged, there is definitely an absolute Christian argument to not only justify but to require that we give protection and assistance in old age. That thought may persuade some who are indifferent as to whether politics are Christian to come to the firm view that it is personally safer if politics do reflect a Christian viewpoint.

This thought was clearly in Aleksandr Solzhenitsyn's mind when, in May 1983, he received the Templeton Foundation Prize for Progress in Religion. In his address he reflected on the situation in his homeland, Russia, and made this statement: 'If I were asked today to formulate as concisely as possible the main cause of the ruinous revolution that swallowed up some 60 million of our people, I could not put it more accurately than to repeat: "Men have forgotten God; that's why all this has happened."'

In politics no one can deny the thrill of the race, but the prize should not be seen as an end in itself. Rather it is an opportunity to promote just causes and by so doing improve the lot of mankind. Politics, to be Christian, must reflect a genuine concern for the unemployed, the homeless and the aged, all those suffering economic or social stress. In other words, the disadvantaged. It must also reflect an appreciation of the unique worth of each individual.

Some may see a contradiction between emphasising the individual and the Christian message of concern for one another. I see no such conflict. Without diminishing the uniqueness of individual but rather because of their intrinsic worth, we have a Christian responsibility to be our brother's keeper. During the course of my speech I have given my answer to the question 'Can politics be Christian?'. I have also set out some arguments and quoted some examples to enable you to make your personal assessment on whether politics can be, are, or should be Christian. For myself as a Christian and as a politician, I repeat the prayer that's on a plaque on my office wall in the Beehive: 'God grant me the serenity to accept the things I cannot change, the courage to change the things I can and the wisdom to know the difference.'

Wellington

On 25 November 1972, the National Party suffered its worst election result in 12 years, losing office to the Labour Party of Norman Kirk. Among the relatively few electoral success stories on the National side was one Jim Bolger, a new MP for the freshly created seat of King Country, who had taken the electorate with a tidy 1240-vote majority. The paucity of new MPs would be to his political advantage, giving him a variety of portfolios that he would later assume when his party won the following election in 1975.

A lot has already been written about his political achievements and activities over this period. Many of the particularly illuminating observations were gathered together in *The Bolger Years*, a volume edited by Professor Margaret Clark. Jim himself has dwelt at length on various policies whose introduction he oversaw in a book published in 1998, *Bolger: A View From the Top*.

What interested me a little more than memories of policies long gone was getting a better sense of the institution he first encountered. How different was Parliament from the one we recognise today? Although the early 1970s was probably the peak era of the post-war public service culture (not counting the number of ostensibly private firms whose main or only contracts were with the government), Parliament was a surprisingly modest affair in terms of financial reward, even more so in terms of required hours. Nor was the Beehive yet an architectural symbol of the executive branch.

Also rather absent from the scene were women. Only a dozen had then made it into a New Zealand Parliament as MPs. Germaine Greer's *The Female Eunuch* may still have been all the rage, but women were locked out of politics. And yet various women would go on to play such a significant part in Jim's own political story.

Managing the intuitive greed of a significant percentage of the population is a challenge for political leaders everywhere. I've been in a position to see it growing as an issue over many decades. 'Greed is good' became something of a catch-cry before the edifice created by that mindset crumbled in the 2008 financial crash.

In a way, I'm probably fortunate because I got into politics in the era I did, when money really wasn't the name of the game. At that time, in the early 1970s, the salary for a backbench MP was $7800, or something like that. The pay was modest but reflected the earlier view that the job itself was seen as part-time. Overwhelmingly, in New Zealand, the early politicians were farmers or people of that cut. They came to Wellington in the winter. Parliament opened in about June and then you went through the winter months. Then in the spring it was back to the farm. It was rather like what we had with the Cooks' and Stewards' Union on the ferries.

That started to change, though, after the Labour government elected in 1972 set up a group to review parliamentary salaries and it recommended a significant increase. The Kirk government also introduced much higher salaries and fees for councillors on local bodies — previously you probably got a free lunch, but not a lot else.

That 1972 election when Kirk became prime minister was a transition time in many other respects. It was — what? — 27 years after the end of World War II, not very long at all, when you think about it, and not that much longer than we are today from the 9/11 attack in New York. In the early 1970s, a high percentage of those in the National Party were also returned servicemen, whereas in the Labour Party there was this huge surge of younger members who came in with the Norman Kirk victory.

This all started the transition of Parliament to being an institution that better reflected society as a whole, a greater diversity of experience. Labour was younger, it had far more women (although nothing like what we have now, and nobody back then was talking about percentage quotas) and there were also Māori members on that side of the House. I don't think there were any at that point from the Pacific Island nations. Certainly there weren't any Asians. But looking back you can definitely see that election was sort of the watershed moment for the old order — the men's club that was Parliament, basically — to the new order, where it was much more a representative body.

Initially, though, that fresh infusion only lasted three years, because there was a great culling in 1975 with the victory of Robert Muldoon, whose win probably delayed the transition to a more representative Parliament. But that transition certainly came. Just look at the institution today and compare it, as I sometimes do, with what it was in the early 1970s when, on our side at least, there was not even a single female MP, and the senior woman on the Labour side was Whetu Tirikatene-Sullivan, the first-ever Māori woman to become a minister.

Four prime ministers: David Lange, Jim Bolger, Sir Robert Muldoon and Mike Moore, photographed in 1992 at Muldoon's valedictory dinner.

What I've just mentioned — the lack of diversity, the shorter hours in Parliament and the small pay packet — started to change when Kirk called the House together in February 1973. February! Lots of people were shocked because Parliament *never* used to be called together until June, which on our side allowed us to get our branch meetings done without the bother of having to travel to Wellington. Sadly, or not, the days of politics in the capital being something of a winter profession were over.

At the same time, our society was changing, too. I suppose it had been from the end of World War I, in 1918, bringing down the curtain on an unending bloodbath that cost millions of lives for little purpose. Which led on to the Great Depression of the 1930s, in which virtually everybody — certainly the average citizen — suffered grave deprivation, adding further misery to the world. The horrors of World War I followed by the Great Depression led to the rise of Hitler, driven in part by the terrible conditions in Germany. Hitler's rise led on to the Holocaust and appalling mass murder of the Jewish people. There was little justification for World War I, but World War II had to be fought to stop Hitler. That war impacted on the whole world and culminated in the use of atomic weapons for the first, and thankfully only, time in history. The death toll was appalling.

What a tumultuous period, and one in which there were just 21 fleeting years between the end of one war and the start of another. The level of madness is hard to contemplate. Off went the sons and daughters — mainly the sons — of the World War I veterans to fight another war, and five years after World War II there was the Korean War and then on to the Vietnam War, which divided New Zealand.

At the 1975 election National brought in two women MPs, the Christchurch accountant Colleen Dewe and the very young Marilyn Waring. They were the fourteenth and fifteenth women ever elected to the New Zealand Parliament. Nowadays there are as many women in Parliament as there were in total over the previous more than 120 years. That statistic tells you much about how our country has changed.

Colleen Dewe remained in Parliament for just the one term, but Marilyn stayed on and would make a bigger impression. Partly that was because of her age — she was just 22 or 23 when she entered the House — but also because of her strength and personal qualities. I got a taste of this early on when I attended her selection meeting in a school hall in Ngāruawāhia. That event itself was illustrative of where the wider culture was going. Four other staunch members of the National Party, all men and all perfectly good people, were vying for the nomination. As each of them dropped off in the progressive ballot system used, some of their votes went to Marilyn, who was an entirely different kind of candidate and also, I have to say, the one who had given the best speech on the night. As we know, she won, much to the surprise of the majority of the people there.

But nobody should have been that surprised. She was a bright young woman who was working in the National Party research unit in Parliament when she decided to seek the nomination for the safe National seat of Raglan, where her parents lived. She clearly offered a different perspective in terms of style and, as it emerged, with more liberal views than I had on some controversial sexually aligned issues. She has been identified with some of those since leaving politics.

You asked about the general feeling when Marilyn was outed in 1976 as a lesbian by the tabloid paper *Truth*. My own feeling is that it didn't come as a surprise. In fact, I remember that other media didn't make half the fuss that *Truth* had made about it. But there were still big historical negatives about gay people, not only women, but men, too. But I think those of us who had some small experience of the world knew that it was a reality of life. And the fact that Marilyn came out as such was not a huge deal. The drama might have been a surprise to some but by no means all.

Marilyn has had a successful career in many fields since she left Parliament. I recently launched her book, *Marilyn Waring: The Political Years*, at Waikato University, where she earned her PhD. It is an interesting and detailed take on her years in Parliament. For me, though, her legacy lives on in the growing significance of the question of how we measure what's important in society. Marilyn has written about this convincingly over the years. She has ridiculed the notion of GDP being the ultimate measure of social wellbeing. Marilyn has especially focused on the unpaid work of women. And as far as I can see, it doesn't take much reflection to say she's absolutely right. The majority of people recognise that the most important job in the world is bringing up the next generation; that is, the job of mothers and motherhood, and that this work and unpaid work in other fields have no value when we measure progress in society only by GDP. That is nonsense. This matter has to be resolved. In a world that professes to be concerned with the environment, we should reflect that cutting down the Amazon forest adds to GDP — and by that measure would be good!

Yet it has taken a long time for the world to start to move on this and we're still a long way from addressing it. I talk about it frequently now, saying we have to have a better measure of what's important than GDP. Although, to be honest, it's much easier to articulate this issue than to provide clear answers as to how it should best be done. But Marilyn was one of the first to clearly raise it. That's where her legacy lies.

I'm not saying she and I were close. She was tighter with other members of Parliament. But there was no antagonism, either; we just moved in different circles. Of course, in 1975, I was a junior minister, a parliamentary undersecretary, and then I became a minister a couple of years later. So that's what I was mainly focused on politically. And feminism wasn't something I'd been exposed to in any particular way. The farming community really should have been a chief activist in this area, given the work that farm wives had done down the centuries to keep the farming industry alive, but they weren't. Unfortunately it wasn't seen as a big deal.

But it didn't take long for me to work out that the political world wasn't doing everything perfectly on many fronts. It's never been difficult for me to see mistakes and errors in the status quo, which I'm not intuitively attracted to anyway. Politics is about a better tomorrow, and you're simply not going to have a better tomorrow if you can't move past the status quo. That's true of any issue.

For me, it comes back to what took me into Parliament, which was, I suppose, what looked like the sheer mayhem in the freezing works and the industrial disputes. I was keen to find new ways around the problems. An early solution that I promoted with others was to develop a new ownership structure in the meat industry and have the unions as part-owners, so they had a vested interest in making sure that the industry worked properly. I was prepared and open to looking at a different approach to an old problem.

A respected local farmer, Ed Buckley, and I had travelled the back roads of the King Country to gain commitments from farmers that they would put up the capital needed to build a cooperative meat works with the union as part shareholders. Unfortunately, the meat industry back then was regulated by the New Zealand Meat Board, and they wouldn't grant the farmers' group I was working with the necessary licence to build a plant. So that idea went nowhere, much to my regret. When I entered Parliament one of the first things I had the National Party commit to was to delicense meat processing plants when we next became government. Which we did.

You wanted to talk about the 1984 election. That's jumping ahead, but let's. I wasn't there on the night the snap election was called. I was returning from the International Labour Organization conference in Geneva, because as well as being New Zealand's minister of labour, in 1983 I was elected president of the ILO, which has existed since the formation of the League of Nations, a tripartite organisation with equal representation from government, employers and union organisations.

I'll tell you a story about the Geneva conference. About 1000 delegates attended, and among the speakers was New Zealand's Federation of Labour leader Jim Knox. As the president, I welcomed him onto the stage to address the large audience. Jim entered with a bit of a scowl, came up to the lectern and said, 'I'm not going to congratulate the president, as all others have done — he has been screwing the workers at home and he's going to screw them again.' He ranted on for quite a while. You could see the audience saying, 'Oh my!'

As the president and chair of the conference I always saw copies of the speeches before they were delivered. I'd read Jim's speech and considered it to be of no great consequence, but then he diverted from his notes halfway through to attack me, again, before returning to the script. And then at the end he just kept on going. The second time, I let him go for quite a little while, and then I banged the gavel and told him, 'Sorry, your time has expired.' He stalked off, declaring in a very loud voice that I was stopping him speaking here,

I was stopping him speaking in New Zealand, and so forth.

You could sense the audience thinking how strange this all was, these two New Zealanders sniping away at each other. As I invited the next speaker up I noticed that Jim had left his glasses behind on the lectern. I asked whether somebody from the New Zealand delegation might like to come up to reclaim Mr Knox's glasses. That sort of cracked the audience up. Things relaxed.

After the conference I travelled home from Geneva through Hong Kong, where I had decided to break the trip. As we were leaving my hotel room to head to the airport for the last leg home, the phone rang and my press secretary Jim Burns went back in and answered it. He came back saying, 'Boss, you'd better come and listen to this because they're talking about a snap election.' The two people on the phone, if memory serves, were Bill Birch and David Thomson. They put the best spin they could on the decision to call the election but I was totally unpersuaded and I can recall my words to them: 'It must look very different from where you are than from where I am. I'll see you in 12 hours.' I've never understood why the caucus went along with Muldoon's proposal.

Thus the snap election. It was sad. The three people who might have spoken up in the caucus to contest the idea were me, George Gair and Hugh Templeton, who were both recovering from cancer operations while I, of course, was abroad. The point is, as far as I know, nobody there was prepared to say, 'What a really *stupid* idea!' And it really was.

At the time, there was a big industrial strike in the oil refinery at Whāngārei, and Jim Knox had said to me more than once when we were in Geneva, 'You're just trying to get a snap election, aren't you?' And I would say, 'Nope, not even the National Party is stupid enough to call a snap election at this stage.' I believed that: I'd seen the polls. And then, lo and behold, before I got home, one was called. I was coming around Oriental Bay from the airport — we were living in Bolton Street at that stage, in the ministerial house — and Rob Muldoon was on the radio in the car talking about Rob's Mob against 'your lot'. I thought, 'Um, that's not a great campaign slogan.'

There had been no preparation, of course, for any election. Sue Wood, our party president, had been apprehensive, or anxious, that something ridiculous was going to happen, and she was right. Jim McLay, the deputy leader, didn't have much input into the election either. Sue Wood and I called in a former Colenso man, Michael Wall, who was a friend of mine and who had worked on campaigns before, to help us to develop a strategy, and Bill Birch also helped. We worked closely with Sue to try to get some sort of a strategy for a campaign. Sue was there the whole time, trying to salvage what you've just described as a 'Theresa May moment' for the party. I mean, only the day before the election was called, the party's national executive had reviewed the party's own polling, which told a disastrous story. We had a good idea of what was in store.

At the same time, David Lange was at the height of his oratory and his popular power, if that's the right term for it. He demolished Muldoon in the television debates. In one of them, with Ian Johnstone as moderator, Rob was reduced to saying at the end, 'And I love you, too, Mr Lange.' It was his admission of surrender, really.

Muldoon used Marilyn, and specifically her support for anti-nuclear legislation, as the reason for calling the early election. My understanding is that she'd guaranteed Muldoon that she'd vote with the National Party on a matter of confidence. In other words, she wouldn't bring the government down. But the accusation is that she did bring the government down. Well, as we know now, the government most certainly went down anyway.

above Jim chipping a piece off the Berlin Wall on a visit to Europe shortly after the Brandenburg Gate was opened on 9 November 1989.

below Jim and his good mate and later finance minister Bill Birch heading off fishing at Snells Beach.

Taking a Global View

New Zealand Institute of International Affairs, 18 September 1990

Three years ago, when I released National's foreign affairs and defence policies for the 1987 election, all attention was focused on how National would deal with the vexed question of potentially nuclear-armed ships entering our ports. No commentators in 1987 concerned themselves one bit with the Gulf region, other than to note how falling oil prices had severely damaged the economic viability of the energy projects constructed by the last National government.

It is remarkable how the world scene has changed in the past three years. The Gulf crisis has almost trebled the price of oil and the energy projects now appear wise investments; the Cold War is over, the Berlin Wall is down, Germany is reunified and New Zealand has a bipartisan policy opposing nuclear weapons in our ports. And Bob Jones wants us to have a defence alliance with the United States!

The message of the last three years as it relates to foreign and defence policies is very clear. The world will not wait for New Zealand. We must reach out to the world. Our policies must be determined on what is in New Zealand's long-term interests and we must actively pursue those interests. This includes both our strategic and trade interests.

For example, in the 1960s it was accepted that it was in New Zealand's long-term interest to retain a trading foothold in Europe after Britain joined the European Community. Considerable effort was required to achieve a positive end result for New Zealand, but the effort has paid big dividends. Europe continues to be a very important market for New Zealand, even though it can be argued that the centre of gravity for New Zealand trade has moved closer to home.

The flow-on effects from Iraq's invasion of Kuwait reach across the world to New Zealand and involve New Zealanders. My sympathy goes out to the New Zealanders caught up with the events in the Gulf and to their families here in New Zealand. From the briefings I have received, I believe the government has taken all possible steps to assist both the New Zealanders in Kuwait and Iraq and their families here in New Zealand. I support those steps.

In policy terms one impact of the Iraqi invasion is to yet again show that New Zealand must take a global view on foreign policy issues and not withdraw to impotent isolation in the south-west Pacific. New Zealand, as a trading nation, is affected by events all around the globe. So, within the limits of our resources, we must retain an interest and, where possible, a presence in strategic capitals and regions.

The present government has correctly offered humanitarian aid to the victims of Saddam Hussein's aggression, and in particular assisting in air-lifting refugees back to their home countries. However, by far the largest share of the burden of containing the expansionist dreams of Saddam Hussein and his million-strong Iraqi army has fallen to the United States.

President Bush has, in my judgement, displayed commendable skill and courage in facing up to another modern dictator. His has been the voice of strength and the voice of reason. Following his leadership, a large number of nations have committed forces to prevent Saddam Hussein moving into Saudi Arabia with the eventual goal of forcing Iraq back within its own borders.

Such is the scale of the change in global alliances, the Soviet Union has committed itself to support the United States and other Western nations in standing up against the Iraqi aggression, an alliance that could not have been conceived only 12 months ago. The importance of the United Nations Security Council's unanimous agreement to the imposition of sanctions against Iraq is also of great significance.

The United Nations by that action came off the fence and aligned itself solidly behind those committed to stopping the expansionist goals of Saddam Hussein. The United Nations will have gained stature from being willing to be strong in the face of naked aggression.

If Saddam Hussein had not been prevented from taking control of Saudi Arabia, he would have controlled nearly one-quarter of Western and Middle Eastern oil production. Such control would have given him enormous leverage over the world's economies, with serious consequences for us.

At this stage, with no clear end in sight, New Zealand must remain ready to make our contribution to defend the rights of small nations if called upon to do so.

Now that the heat has gone out of the nuclear debate in New Zealand, we need to take a cooler view of New Zealand's foreign policy objectives and the requirement for New Zealand to have friends and allies around the world. The crisis in the Persian Gulf has been a sobering reminder that events half a world away impact directly and adversely on our lives and that New Zealand cannot be indifferent to world events.

I therefore strongly reject the trend that has emerged in the six years of Labour government for New Zealand to become more inward-looking and insular. If such a trend was to continue it would lead New Zealand down the path to international irrelevance, and make the achievement of our trading objectives that much more difficult.

It is against this background that the National Party has shaped its foreign and defence policies with the aim of taking New Zealand into the next century as a respected and active participant in the international community.

New Zealand's area of immediate strategic and political concern is the South Pacific. The South Pacific Forum remains the single most important body in our immediate region and provides the focus for addressing the mutual concerns of our Pacific neighbours.

Under National, New Zealand will continue its active membership of the forum as well as representing, as appropriate, the interests of the small island nations in the larger world arena.

The forum nations will also continue as the primary focus of our development assistance which we will increase as our own economic situation improves. Under National, we will provide help and assistance to the greatest extent possible to our Pacific Island country friends. Not only do they live in our strategic area, but because of significant migration from the Pacific to New Zealand, Pacific Islanders are now a significant minority group within New Zealand itself. They are now making a contribution to New Zealand in a wide range of areas. Their contribution is most welcome.

I reject the notion, however, that New Zealand is only a South Pacific nation. I advance instead the view we are a Pacific nation which, through background, culture and trade, has not only Pacific interests but also global interests.

New Zealand's single most important trading and security partner is our trans-Tasman neighbour, Australia. Our trade links with Australia are too numerous to count but they bind our two economies together in a fashion that will deepen and grow further over the years.

When it was clear that earlier trade arrangements would outlive their usefulness, the National government in the early 1980s set about negotiating a new trading relationship with Australia. Those negotiations culminated with the signing of the Closer Economic Relations agreement in 1983, by the Muldoon government — not the Labour government or Mike Moore, as he likes to claim. The agreement was negotiated with the Liberal government of Malcolm Fraser, but because of a change of government in Australia the agreement was actually signed by current Australian prime minister Bob Hawke. Almost immediately New Zealand's exports increased to the extent they were close to parity with Australia's by 1986. Since that signing in 1983, the worth of the CER has been demonstrated many times. It has been shown possible to speed up the original timetable and to bring the almost total integration of our economies at an earlier date.

While the CER has been a success story, it should not hide the fact that there are still a number of issues that remain outstanding. There are issues that an incoming National government would want to raise with its Australian counterpart. We would, for example, seek a greater harmonisation of investment policies and commercial law. This would include full reciprocity for Air New Zealand to fly within Australia just as the Australian airline, Ansett, flies within New Zealand. We would expect substantial movement on these issues leading up to the 1992 review of the agreement.

So there is much detailed work yet to be done on issues affecting the trading relationship between New Zealand and Australia, but this is simply part of the unique and enduring relationship our two countries have — we even let them beat us at rugby a couple of times just to keep up their spirits!

While New Zealand is a Pacific nation, very many New Zealanders have strong cultural ties with Europe. As I travelled through Europe from Moscow to Berlin earlier this year, there was a feeling of a new dawn, the beginning of a new era.

The Cold War was over, the Berlin Wall — that symbol of all that was obscene and divisive in Europe after the Second World War — was being torn down. Standing beside the Wall, and chipping off a symbolic piece, I could not help but try and visualise what the next stage in Europe's turbulent history might turn up.

The totalitarian governments of Eastern Europe have fallen under the irresistible call for democratic revolution. And the Soviet Union itself is under strain as once independent republics that were forcefully included in the union are again demanding their independence.

The scale of historic developments in Europe are hard to overestimate. Since the October Revolution of 1917, the believers in communism have argued an alternative economic and social strategy to that of the market economies. The dream of a new utopia has now vanished, torn down by years of failure, of misguided central planning and the denial of individual rights.

Ironically, as the Soviet and East European economies have abandoned central planning as a failure and embraced a more market approach, Mike Moore's Labour government, as of 17 September, is heading back to central planning — one of the great political U-turns in New Zealand's history. The New Zealand Labour government now joins Albania with its support of state centralist planning. The Europe of the post-war era has gone and none will mourn its passing.

New Zealand has a keen interest in the politics of Europe, given the cultural ties of many New Zealanders to the countries of that continent, but we have a more immediate tie to Europe in terms of trade. Together the 12 member states of the European Community remain New Zealand's most important export market. It is a key market for butter and sheep meat, and is also important for products like apples, kiwifruit and leather.

With internal barriers in the Community due to disappear in 1992, we must ensure we are well positioned to take advantage of the opportunities this major economic power offers. There will, therefore, always be a New Zealand presence in the key capitals of Europe.

Because of the British connection, London remains very important, but much of the business of Europe now centres on Brussels. Germany's massive economic power is likely to increase as the dust settles on unification and we have to ensure we are appropriately represented there. We must also increase our contact with the newer members of the European Community, like Spain, as they exert increasing influence. It is clear Europe will remain very important to New Zealand as a trading partner for the foreseeable future.

Closer to home, we have witnessed massive growth rates in East Asia over the last decade. East Asia's share of the world trade grew steadily from 14 per cent in 1980 to 22 per cent by 1988. That massive growth is reflected in the fact that Asia now takes over one-third of our exports, compared with less than one-quarter for Europe.

Japan has been recognised for some years as a major and growing market, but replicating its success are countries like South Korea, Singapore, Hong Kong and Taiwan. Further trading opportunities do exist in those countries and other Asian countries, and New Zealand businesses will need to pursue them aggressively because the battle to retain market share in Europe will get tougher as competition from Eastern Europe increases. The markets of Asia must be targeted as key growth opportunities for New Zealand and our representation in the region must reflect that fact.

National will also give attention to New Zealand's relationship with its long-standing friend and former ally, the United States. I am sad to have to say former ally, but that happens to be the official position at this time. My goal is to change that.

We all know what caused the problem: the challenge is to find a solution. The only way that can be achieved is by constructive dialogue and good will on both sides.

On being elected the National government will at an early date set out to open up discussions with Washington on how best to make progress, given the now bipartisan commitment to keep nuclear weapons out of New Zealand. My aim is to re-establish a mutually acceptable defence and security relationship. I am confident that with a positive attitude from both sides progress will be made and my goal achieved. The new National government will approach the task with a feeling of goodwill towards the United States and American people.

The key difference between National and Labour on this and other issues is that National rejects any moves to take New Zealand down the path of non-alignment and ultimate neutralism. Small we may be but we are prepared to play our part and carry our share of the burden of maintaining international peace and security.

That approach has shaped National's defence policy. While the emphasis of our foreign policy is more global in its approach, our defence policy, by necessity, must be regional in focus.

Apart from the two world wars, New Zealand has only ever invested to maintain minimum credible defence forces. That goal has served us well, providing both a base on which to expand in time of major conflict and a corps of professional service personnel who could be deployed to meet any lower to medium level emergency in our area of immediate strategic interest — the Australasian–South Pacific region.

To meet New Zealand's widest security requirements successful governments have, until 1984, accepted the need to maintain collective security arrangements, with the major reliance being placed on ANZUS. Because of the Labour government's actions ANZUS is now inoperative. I have already set out my goal to again achieve a mutually acceptable security arrangement with the United States, and I feel sure ANZUS can play a key role in such arrangements.

National believes New Zealand must have defence forces capable primarily of undertaking an effective role in maintaining peace and security in the South Pacific. We accept that resource constraints limit our ability to maintain forces capable of acting independently in anything other than a low-level military emergency of a civil defence/ disaster relief role. New Zealand, therefore, needs to cooperate with other like-minded nations.

For New Zealand the focus of defence effort must be to develop and maintain the capability to operate effectively for a prolonged period in a lower-level threat situation in our area of immediate strategic concern. In addition we must be able to make an appropriate contribution with Australia and other like-minded nations in defence of peace and security in the Pacific or elsewhere, should the need arise.

For this reason it is necessary for the New Zealand forces to keep an expansion capability. The reserves and territorials remain essential for the reinforcement and expansion of the small professional force. To achieve that readiness a concerted effort must be made to shape defence organisation, management and spending to focus on two key elements: the Ready Reaction Force backed by the appropriate air and surface support units, and maritime forces capable of actively patrolling our region to secure the interests and resources of New Zealand and our partners in the South Pacific Forum. Having determined the role of our defence forces, it is critical to ensure that they be of the highest professional standard.

To this end a career structure, involving training at home and abroad, will be emphasised. Such arrangements will provide important training and career development opportunities for our armed forces personnel. This interaction with other forces will ensure that ours are more effective, whether deployed independently or with other nations' forces, and whether deployed for peacekeeping or in combat.

That capability can only be maintained if our defence forces are adequately equipped, particularly in the large capital equipment items. In conjunction with this focusing of defence effort there will, under a National government, be a parallel commitment within the existing defence vote to acquire and renew essential capital equipment. National will therefore honour the contract to purchase the two Anzac frigates ordered from Australia.

National's foreign policy commitment to international peace-keeping and peace-making efforts has already been mentioned. New Zealand has a long and distinguished history of involvement in peacekeeping activities around the world. This role is more likely to increase than diminish. It is an area where New Zealand can make an active contribution to global peace and stability. Present commitments will be continued.

We have come a long way since we looked to Britain as our sole source of wealth, and political and security support. There is much that New Zealanders can be proud of, not least a greater confidence in ourselves as people.

As we look to the next three years — with a single European market, the successful conclusion, we hope, of the GATT Uruguay Round, and a peaceful settlement, we earnestly pray, to the Gulf crisis — New Zealand cannot avoid being affected whatever we do.

Getting out there, however — into Europe, into East Asia, into the Pacific rim — will help to ensure that what happens will be in our best interests. We may be a small player but we can be a constructive player on the world scene. It is my intention that we shall be.

Ninth Floor

An odd claim but, to the best of my knowledge, true: I think I may be the only journalist in New Zealand history to have accidentally named a Budget. This is how it happened. On the morning of 20 February 1991 — the time and date are easy to recall because it was only a few hours after my first son was born — I arrived at the Beehive to interview Jim's then right-hand woman, finance minister Ruth Richardson, for the *Evening Post*. I was told she would be a bit late. I ended up sitting out in the reception area for a while, leafing through the pile of *Economist* magazines that Ruth always made a point of having on the table. Naturally, as the world was still in the midst of the first Gulf war, some of the articles were about Iraq's then defiant leader, Saddam Hussein, and his vow to prosecute the 'mother of all battles' against the US-led coalition looking to displace his army from Kuwait.

I was still reading about it when Ruth finally appeared. She scolded me, in a friendly sort of way, for coming along for an interview so soon after having a child. 'How's the mother?' she asked, and I said she was doing fine, thanks, and then

I quipped, 'And how's the Mother of all Budgets looking?' She said she liked the line, which also found its way into my subsequent article — and became the informal name of that year's Budget.

The austerity plan, as it essentially turned out to be, would also prove to be the mother of all headaches for Jim during his first term as prime minister. Certainly, it was one of the things that most threatened to overshadow what was otherwise an impressively *West Wing*-style professional administration in which Jim figured as a kind of chairman of the board.

So what did that kind of corporate arrangement practically mean? Leadership, Jim still likes to say, essentially comes down to making difficult choices, which I suppose is essentially what the philosopher Karl Popper was getting at when he said that all life is problem solving. Given his labour minister background, which by definition was about finding workable resolutions that various parties would not agree to on their own, Jim's style of business probably wasn't so surprising. Still, it's not something he has talked about a great deal over the years. It seemed like a good theme for our next Friday conversation, which began with a bit of scene-setting about the old media days and extended to reveries about the Richardson relationship — and more about the other woman, Jenny Shipley, who would replace him as party leader.

The media part of being prime minister never used to worry me. It was slightly different in a few respects, though. What we didn't have in the 1990s was these quasi-interviews on the run into Parliament or while walking across to the Beehive. It certainly wasn't common. I'm not sure who started it here. Perhaps they're borrowing from Donald Trump, because Trump's interviews now are nearly always done as he is getting into a helicopter or getting out of it. It's as if they've virtually done away with media conferences, or what in Washington used to be called the press briefings.

You could get a job over there as the new press secretary, David—they come and go, mind. It mightn't be a permanent position. Also, hopefully he doesn't decide that an Iranian war would be beneficial politically, because I think that's a huge worry, and that would make your position stressful.

Trump really does seem to have an absolute hatred of Iran. I don't know why. People like John Bolton, the former national security advisor, seemed to be itching for a war. On the one hand, people say a nuclear-armed Iran would be a problem. I agree, but any nuclear-armed nation is a problem. No, we don't want more. But how about getting the current club members to start to lower their nuclear stockpiles? It really seems that what you've got is a sort of master/servant relationship in which the nations who got in first have these weapons and now say to the rest of the world that they're not safe to have them, but they'll come to no harm if looked after by the current custodians. I find no comfort in that scenario at all.

And now there's Saudi Arabia wanting to join the nuclear club. Saudi Arabia! The Brits have sold a whole lot of technology to the Saudis, who of course are favoured by the West. You have to believe that they scatter their money generously indeed to those who have influence, because, as I've told you, after 9/11, every plane was grounded in America except those of the US military and the Saudis, the latter so that they could pick up important Saudi nationals in the US. To have that influence in such circumstances tells you something. We saw a similar reaction in 2018 in the wake of the murder of journalist Jamal Khashoggi. The UN has come out and said it's clear what happened in the Saudi Arabian embassy in Turkey, but Saudi Arabia declares it didn't sanction the crime. And the Brits and the Americans support the Saudis. Anyhow, that's not part of our discussion today, even if, thanks to the current world leadership, the time feels closer to a serious war than we've been for a long time.

It's difficult to pigeonhole what makes a good leader. Successful leaders obviously have the capacity to deal with many issues differently, according to the matter and according to the circumstances of the moment, and also according to the mood of the electorate. I don't think there's one style of leader that's more impressive than all the others. In politics, what leaders have to be able to do is to give confidence to the caucus, plainly, and to the wider party. But also there's the capacity to see the issues they should be fighting, debating, pursuing, promoting. Because that's the main thing from the country's perspective. The differences in style probably go to those who do their homework and those who get others to do homework. In other words, there's planning in it. Rather than the 'Well, I know I can bullshit my way through' sort of thing.

Take Helen Clark. Helen was never a bombastic leader. It just wasn't her style. She was a careful, thoughtful leader who normally kept the issues clear in her mind. She was quite controlling, I believe, in terms of her caucus, but it never appeared as if she tried to win an argument by brute personality or bombastic speeches alone. She brought her own style to the podium and to the leadership of the country, which again appeared to be about getting the facts, getting the detail, getting her team to produce the data, and then putting it out in a manner that was acceptable and understood. That's what a modern society requires. It's certainly what I tried to do. For me, too, debating was always a strength.

Even before I went into Parliament, I always liked to have the facts. I tried to see where the next story was likely to be. I liked to see around the corner rather than just concentrate on the matters just in front of me. That works at times, and doesn't work at others; and if you're too far in front of the audience, then they don't follow you. I feel as if I was a chairman of the board as well as leader, but a chairman who held strong views, which indeed most successful chairmen do.

So it's a balance. In politics, there's a capacity to rouse an audience with a stirring speech, but also the challenge of commanding attention with a thoughtful presentation. What I always tried to do, as I say, was to see where the next step was, to deal with the issues that had to be dealt with immediately, but to see past that, and that meant being prepared to challenge the status quo. In fact for me it goes without saying that if you're not challenging the status quo you're not searching for better answers.

How does one do it? Partly it's intuition. And how does one get that? I honestly don't know. Maybe you're born with it. I don't know where it comes from, but I do know you need to have it for successful leadership. And what you also don't need is 'Yes Ministers', or rather 'Yes Prime Ministers'. My ministers were willing to come and talk to me if they felt I was straying or not attending to a particular issue of the moment. That never worried me at all. After all, one of the challenges of leaders is how you utilise the talent within your team. And that talent is always going to be mixed, clearly, and you're trying to match a skill base and a capacity to work with the various portfolios. What we used to do, and it's now moving away from this, is try to group portfolios much closer. A minister would be working in a more confined area. Whereas now it seems that ministers have a huge breadth of part portfolios, associate portfolios, something else portfolios. Which doesn't appeal to me at all, to be honest.

It's sort of a grab bag, quite illogical, and not utilising what they're intuitively capable of doing as well as their experience and professional training. I saw Doug Kidd the other day. We were talking about the first treaty settlement we did when Doug was the minister of fisheries, the Sealord deal in 1992, a full and final settlement of related commercial claims. Sealord was the quickest deal we ever did. Why? Because I brought in the leaders Sir Graham Latimer, Sir Tipene O'Regan and Sir Robert Mahuta, as well as my young Maori Affairs advisor, Peter Douglas, to my office for a long night of discussion and negotiation, with both Doug Kidd and Doug Graham coming in at various times to join us. That's how we put together the basis of that agreement. Months of detailed work followed, but the basis of the deal was agreed to in one long night. The detailed work of allocating a particular share of the resource to individual iwi we left for iwi leadership to determine. I still believe that was the right approach.

That's what I mean by intuitive reaction. Doug Kidd had a good understanding of treaty issues. He saw an opportunity. He brought it to my attention. We did it. That's the sort of approach you want from ministers, that they can see opportunities to make progress. Because you don't want ministers who are only intent on propping up the status quo. I've never been interested in that. You want ministers who can see a better tomorrow, actually a different tomorrow, in whatever part of the whole organisation they happen to be in — and yes, it's always a gamble to see who works out well and who doesn't. You always have your disappointments.

Helen Clark didn't take big risks. She had a quite clear philosophical base, which was conservative left in most things other than social issues. That fits in reasonably happily with a high percentage of New Zealanders, so she was comfortable being in front of audiences. Of course, Helen grew up in a farming family in Te Pahu, not that far from where we farmed in the King Country. You say we both could have ended up in the other party? I think she'd disagree with that, and I'd disagree with that, too, but I can see what you're saying. What we both did try to do was have a rational position on issues and not just an ideological position.

We were both the children of farmers, who are a reasonably pragmatic bunch. They have to be. If you're farming, you know you don't control everything, most notably the weather and international prices, so you have to have these other skills to navigate the negatives from time to time. I think this kind of background inculcates a certain realism in what you can or can't predict with great accuracy; in a general direction, yes, but you have to be able to cope with the interruptions. For me, a lot of these considerations were in play when

I had to make a decision as to whether we would formally agree with the non-nuclear policy that the Labour Party had brought in.

I remember once speaking as prime minister to a large group of economists in Singapore. At the end of the meeting somebody asked me about New Zealand's engagement with Asia given that, as he saw it, we were so far away. And I said to the questioner that if, through history, your main trading partners were in Europe, then from my perspective, Asia was close and New Zealand already was part of Asia. Well, that short clip was played endlessly in New Zealand. People told me to get a map! But in fact, if they'd got a map themselves, they would have seen we're far more a part of Asia than we were in Europe. That was probably one of the big turning points. A simple thing like that. People then started to think about our position in the world and where we were. Of course, now we send about 3 or 5 per cent of our exports to Britain and a third to China, which is our largest market.

Partly, I think, leading comes through changing one's focus. Not even changing one's mind. The focus. You have to move it. On the trade front, which is just one example of this, it was facing the reality that we had to put more attention into the new Asia-led order that was emerging, and part of it emerged because of Britain going into the European Union.

A chairman of the board approach to leadership suggests keeping things tidy. It suggests being professional. And that's true. I liked my ministers to be on top of their issues. I liked the senior advisory staff to be the best there were. In that sense, yes, they were a professional group. Likening the PM's style to somebody running a corporate board is a reasonable outsider's observation. I hadn't put it into my mind that way. I think we did have a good, professional group. The Prime Minister's Department went well with Simon Murdoch leading it. He was a very able public servant, the best I've ever dealt with. My

Sir Douglas Graham and Jim with Sir Robert Mahuta and Te Arikinui Dame Te Atairangikaahu at Tūrangawaewae Marae after signing the Tainui settlement in May 1995. The Treaty of Waitangi settlement process would become one of Jim's most enduring points of political pride.

private office was very ably led by my chief of staff, Robert Eaddy, who was my right-hand man for over 11 years. Another person who kept the office moving was Paul Plummer, who was born in Granity, on the West Coast. He was always willing to inject some humour into a tense moment. Both remain close friends. On the media front we had a number of very skilled individuals. My friend Jim Burns was with me before and after I became prime minister and remains a close friend, as was the late David Beatson, who I also recruited when I was leader of the Opposition. He was a tremendously good, certainly the best, speechwriter I had in the sense that he could pick up the nuances of my thinking to put into draft notes. Therese Anders, who had spent many years in South Africa and spoke Afrikaans, was very helpful when we attended the inauguration of Nelson Mandela. Mandela was a truly remarkable person and friend. The world needs more like him. Another friend, Michael Wall, was with me for a long period. Richard Griffin, the long-time political voice of RNZ, joined me towards the end. They and others were all essential parts of the team. The prime minister doesn't work alone.

I mentioned Helen Clark earlier because if you go back to the Lange era, you see a prime minister being almost entirely subsumed by Roger Douglas, changing his mind dramatically and embracing neoliberalism, and turning Labour Party policy on its head and embracing policy many saw as to the right of the National Party. And being proud to do so. There was such a chasm between what he said before that 1984 election and what he did afterwards, in particular his subservience to Douglas and his economic policies and pursuits before the 1987 financial crash brought it all to an end. Looking back, the Rogernomics era lasted little more than three years.

Ironically, if we hadn't had the snap election in July 1984, which brought the electoral cycle forward by a few months, then the 1987 election would have been held after the '87 October financial crash. Almost certainly that would have been a three-year Labour government rather than a six-year one. It wouldn't have been too different to the one-term Kirk–Rowling era. The unanswered question for many is, would Labour have succeeded in 1975 if it hadn't been for Kirk's unexpected and sudden death? So Helen's was really the first stable Labour-led government, probably since the first one in the 1930s, since the Savage and Fraser era.

Other Labour leaders in their own time were different, too. Geoffrey Palmer had other skills. I think he found being prime minister really difficult. That's not belittling him. He's got many, many skills and is still a big contributor in other areas, but I don't think being prime minister was ever going to be a part of that. Clearly the Labour Party decided as much when they replaced him after a few months. And I don't think Mike Moore was ever going to be a successful long-term prime minister, either. He was too volatile.

In the era of Donald Trump, though, that might have worked; Mike was certainly volatile enough in his positions and his presentations, but the New Zealand electorate wasn't going to buy that. In Washington I worked with him to gain the support of the US in his and New Zealand's campaign for him to become the director-general of the World Trade Organization. So in terms of Labour leaders, in positive terms, that's Fraser, Savage and Clark. David Lange as prime minister certainly gave New Zealand profile, with his erudite defence of New Zealand's anti-nuclear position in the Oxford Union debate. I said at the time all New Zealanders could be proud of the performance. I think historically that's it.

Was there any similarity between the Lange–Douglas dynamic and my relationship with Ruth Richardson? Not at all. Yes, Ruth certainly had clear views on economics, but there was never the Roger Douglas dominance thing going on. Not at all. People often ask why I replaced her as minister of finance after the 1993 election. The 1993 election was a major pivot point for New Zealand. The referendum to introduce the MMP voting system was chosen by the electorate, meaning that all future governments would be coalition governments. I didn't believe that Ruth could intuitively make the necessary compromises that would be inevitable if we were to work collaboratively in a coalition government. I know Ruth didn't agree with me, of course, and she resigned, despite being offered other important portfolios.

But that's life and it's worth recalling, and if National had lost the subsequent by-election for Ruth's seat then the National government would have lost its tiny majority and been back to the Opposition and much of Ruth's work would have been thrown out by a Labour-led government. We moved on. Bill Birch took the finance portfolio, working on it with his normal, thorough, detailed, sensible perspective. Bill also had to step up once before when I came back from an overseas trip and moved him to the health portfolio. He had also successfully navigated the controversial Employment Contracts Act through as minister of labour. Bill was not only a good friend but also a very good minister.

I first met Ruth when she was a legal counsel with Federated Farmers, so I knew who she was and welcomed her when she came into politics. She was, in general, strongly supportive of Rogernomics, which made life a little difficult because its author was on the other side of the House. She was a committed believer in the markets having the capacity to answer all issues; the government's role was to facilitate the markets to deliver the best possible answer.

I had a much more cynical — sceptical might be a better word — view on that philosophy. I still do. While the market is a powerful adjudicator, history has shown that the markets also leave out large parts of society, which in turn leads to a variety of unpleasant developments: for instance, the 1918 Bolshevik revolution in Russia.

So Ruth and I weren't fully in lockstep on political economic philosophy. Despite that, though, I thought the clarity of her thinking would be beneficial. That's why I made her minister of finance, a role she held for three years and through which she introduced a rigour into economic debate that was certainly beneficial. Ruth had quite a lot of support in caucus. But her rigid views on a lot of matters weren't conducive, in my mind, to working in a coalition relationship.

Did I have reservations? Well, I guess I had reservations every time I appointed somebody, but I had positive expectations, too. I was just hoping that those expectations would come to pass. But my daily working relationship with her ran perfectly well. There were debates on tax policy between her and the revenue minister, Wyatt Creech, and I had to arbitrate on those from time to time. But I had to arbitrate on other ministers' disagreements as well.

I also knew that I would have to keep myself closely involved. Interestingly enough, one of the enduring pieces of legislation passed in my time as PM was the Fiscal Responsibility Act, a joint piece of legislation put together by Ruth and me to make sure that governments had to tell the truth before each election on the state of the economy. We did that in the wake of inheriting the mess we did, the extent of which wasn't made clear until the day after the 1990 election, when senior officials in effect demanded to see me to set out the true state of the economy. Within hours of that briefing I had called Ruth, Bill Birch and Don McKinnon to Wellington to put together a rescue package for the Bank of New Zealand. That was something we worked on closely, and we really didn't have any disagreements. The Rogernomics approach certainly didn't work for BNZ.

It's funny. If we had been totally consistent with the line about the markets always delivering the right answer, we wouldn't have rescued the BNZ at all. In that sense at least, Ruth was a pragmatist when the issues were big enough. She certainly didn't oppose us rescuing BNZ. But in a pure market economy, BNZ would have crashed. It would have been chaotic. Huge social harm. But we didn't do that. Although Ruth was normally a most active supporter of the market knowing best, she was smart enough also to know its limits. To me it has been very interesting to watch businesses and corporate leaders, normally strong supporters of the 'market knows best' view, putting their collective hands out for government support when the Covid-19 virus swept across the world.

In terms of leaders, National has had a few interesting individuals, starting from its formation out of the amalgamation of the Liberal and the Conservative parties in 1936. The first National Party prime minister was Sid Holland. I didn't ever meet him but his son, Eric, was in Parliament when I arrived. He was followed by Keith Holyoake, who won four elections — a remarkable effort. Keith was still in Parliament when I arrived and I enjoyed many chats with him, and learnt much from him. He was followed by John Marshall, who is better remembered as a successful foreign and trade minister than as a prime minister. John was leader when I entered Parliament, but he was soon replaced by Robert Muldoon after the 1972 election defeat.

Rob Muldoon was a distinctive leader and because of that for some

Jim, his finance minister Ruth Richardson, future political rival Jenny Shipley, and minister of women's affairs Katherine O'Regan in 1993, planting a tree on the 100th anniversary of New Zealand women getting the vote — the first women in the world to do so.

a divisive leader. His natural aggression when under pressure was not an endearing feature of his style, but he had more ability than most to bring the details of complex issues together in a succinct form. I didn't support his divisive style but in general we got along well. He occasionally interfered on complex industrial relations issues, which I didn't enjoy, and I made my view clear more than once.

After Muldoon lost the 1984 election the caucus moved fairly quickly to elect a new leader. There were really only two names: Jim McLay and Jim Bolger. We both stood for the leadership of the party in 1984 and Jim McLay won and I was elected unopposed as his deputy. The view was that the caucus wanted someone who was a distinct break from the Muldoon era, and when Jim was elected I offered him my full support. A year or so into Jim's term as leader, a representative group of caucus came to me and asked me to run for leader. I said that if the majority of caucus wanted me to be the leader, then they would have to organise it. I didn't intend to organise a coup. I had given my support to McLay when he won the ballot.

Anyhow, they came back to me two or three weeks later and said, 'There's a clear majority that want you to take over as leader.' That's what happened. Jim's stint at the top wasn't successful in the mind of the majority of his caucus. George Gair was first elected as my deputy and we worked well together. After we lost the 1987 campaign Don McKinnon became my deputy and was an excellent choice. Don and I worked well together, and he was, importantly, a successful foreign minister when the world community was going through the beginning of a realignment with China. Don went on to be a successful secretary-general of the Commonwealth.

Bill English, on the other hand, I thought of as my heir apparent. He came in in 1990. I was impressed with his work ethic. He was so hard-working as a backbencher and had such a clear mind. He had the potential to go all the way. The heir apparent thing didn't quite work that way, although he eventually got there, becoming prime minister for a short while, after a long and convoluted journey. But he always had that ability. People really saw it in the 2017 election, unlike the appalling (from a National Party point of view) 2002 election and then the troubled period that followed with Don Brash. Don came close to winning in 2005. He was ideological in most things, as has become more and more apparent. So it was to the good fortune of the National Party that John Key had been elected when he was, in 2002, and was there to step up and take the party forward for the next three terms from 2008. John had a successful time as leader and PM. If Bill had been able to put together a coalition after the 2017 election, I believe that a key focus of his term would have been to rethink how we deliver welfare support. I'm sure that he would have wanted to do that in a manner that encouraged recipients to develop or acquire the skills they needed to enable them to become independent. Bill is someone who is capable of thinking outside the box.

These transition periods are challenging. From my experience in working with him when he was minister of energy, Simon Bridges is a perfectly good person and he was a good minister, but he was unable to get cut-through with the electorate just as, three years earlier, Andrew Little was unable to get cut-through and was replaced as Labour leader by Jacinda Ardern. This time it was National's turn to make a late change in leader when they elected Todd Muller to lead them into the election. I've known Todd for many years. He worked in my office for three years when I was prime minister. Todd is able and smart and, importantly, he has shown that on key issues like climate change he is able and willing to work across party lines when appropriate and in New Zealand's interests. New Zealand needs these skills at this time as we collectively work to get the economy up and running again, to increase employment and to reduce the numbers relying on welfare support to survive.

This is not a case of trying to recreate yesterday's economy. That can't be done. It's much more about changing focus and seeing the economy as a 'tool' rather than an end point in and of itself — a tool that can be deployed to enable society to achieve the fair and balanced community that all but a few want. In the recent past the economy has been deployed in a manner that has enabled the very few to accumulate vast wealth while the majority struggled. Given the current instability in many countries it would be wise to call to mind the words of Aristotle: 'Inequality is the chief cause of revolution.' Looking across the world, gross inequality raises its head everywhere — including in New Zealand. The coronavirus has already caused a revolution on a scale no one would have contemplated a few months back, including strict controls on everyone's civil rights. Looking forward, no matter who leads the next government, more focus is required on policies to reduce inequality. A minor revolution that could come to pass is for a Todd Muller-led National Party to form a coalition government with a Winston Peters-led New Zealand First. I formed such a government after the 1996 election, which was going well until Jenny Shipley took over as prime minister and it soon collapsed.

I don't know how many 'mini' coalition agreements I signed with people going out to form their own party. What we had in New Zealand after the 1993 referendum which supported a move to MMP was two or three groups of National MPs setting up to become that pivot party that could go either way and be part and parcel of the government almost forever. The German model. All sorts of people headed off to do just that, which made it a challenging time to hold a government and caucus all facing in the right direction.

Then there was Winston Peters. Winston was in my first Cabinet as

Maori Affairs minister and I was expecting, hoping, that he would put his considerable skills to developing policies focused on lifting the achievement and outcomes for Māori. Unfortunately during his time in my first Cabinet he often went out on an issue contrary to party policy and was disloyal to the party on a regular basis. I put up with it for a long time but eventually I told Winston that I was reshuffling the Cabinet and he wouldn't be in it. As history records, he went out and started New Zealand First, which to me is a local populist version of Donald Trump's Make America Great Again, but, having said that, Winston in my view has far better developed political skills than Trump and has been a successful minister of foreign affairs. Maybe I should have given him that portfolio first!

But he's done well. He was out for one term, but he clearly is enormously influential in Jacinda Ardern's government. Winston himself has now found a different niche in the political spectrum. I chat with him infrequently, but whenever we do there's no difficulty chewing the fat on current issues.

Jenny Shipley's tenure as leader was short and unsuccessful as she lost the next election by a big margin. My colleagues never told me exactly why they wanted to change the leader when they did, so I can't really tell you with any certainty what it is they were seeking, why they wanted Jenny. But it didn't work. Jenny was quite a different person to Ruth, although I think they were quite close, not least because of the obvious Canterbury connection. Jenny was a capable minister but I never saw her as my successor. She was competent and she handled most things well. That's why she was a minister in my Cabinet, which I tried to make much more diverse than the scene I described back in the 1970s.

I was looking to balance the National Party's presentation to the world. Yes, we still had a very small number of women MPs at that stage. The good news now is that it's a much more balanced caucus, not near 50 per cent yet, but compared with when I started and where it is now, a lot of progress has been made. That also made Jenny an automatic choice to go into my first Cabinet. There was no debate on that. But I was surprised that caucus thought that she was the solution to whatever they thought their problem was. Maybe it would have been better to discuss it with me. I mean, it took them another four leaders to find someone who could win an election — and I'd just won three.

I was overseas when the coup happened, at the Commonwealth Heads of Government Meeting in Edinburgh, and then in Paris — the first official visit to Paris by a New Zealand prime minister — where I laid a wreath at the Tomb of the Unknown Soldier at the Arc de Triomphe after dark. I don't recall why we were so late. After my official duties were completed we set off for home with no inkling of the plotting that had been going on in Wellington while we were away. It has always surprised me that no one called and gave me a heads up on the plotting.

When we landed in Auckland and came in through arrivals I saw my good friend Doug Graham there to meet me. He said we needed to talk. We moved away a little while the bags were being sorted and he gave me the lowdown on what was happening. He said that they were confident they had the numbers.

I thought it was a huge mistake, obviously. But it wasn't just ego. I knew as much as anyone that it was going to be hard to win the next election, to win a fourth term. The plotters claimed they had the numbers. Maybe so. I had one or two colleagues, especially Paul East, a perceptive friend and ministerial colleague, saying 'Well, we should test that, Jim.' And I thought, 'No, bugger it.' I was tired. I'd just come back from the other side of the world. I'd been working hard for the party for years. If that's what they do when I'm out of the country, I thought, I'll leave them to run it themselves and see how good they are.

So why did it happen? I sometimes wonder if it had something to do with a series of speeches I gave to the party's regional conferences in 1997 in which, instead of just attacking the Opposition, I set out a new concept to address many community issues. I called it 'social capital', utilising the community to offer solutions to their own issues, from unemployment to homelessness. It was an idea that was being advanced by Professor Robert Putman at Harvard University, whom I later met when I was in Washington. I think some in the caucus thought I had wandered too far away from bread-and-butter issues. Maybe someone will venture into that space again. I hope so because we must engage the community if we are to have permanent solutions. But no, I wasn't angry at the plotters. It was more like frustration that they were so naïve to do what they were doing. If they wanted to have a new leader and they had a rational reason, they would have been wise to come and talk to me. I'd actually been leader for nearly 12 years. I did know a little bit about it. But that's politics.

I tried to stay professional during the remaining time I spent in Parliament, which actually wasn't very long. I spent much of that time writing my first book, *A View From the Top*. I effectively appointed myself to Washington. I wanted to get out of the road — which is to say, I didn't want to do a Rob Muldoon and keep hanging around and offering advice from the sidelines. Ambassador to Washington seemed like a fascinating post, especially as I knew that there was a presidential election coming up. I've always taken an interest in American politics. New Zealand had some big issues we had to deal

above Mike Moore offering congratulations after Jim put together a coalition government with Winston Peters after the 1996 election.

below Cartoonist Tom Scott's take on the Shipley coup.

with, with America. I thought I'd probably deal with them as well as anybody else.

Now John Key was interesting. He had a natural, easy, welcoming persona. He played that leadership role well. He reached across divides. He had a soft word on most issues. He led New Zealand through some difficult times, including the financial crash of 2008 and the terrible Christchurch earthquakes. His departure a year before the triennial election was a surprise to me. Clearly he'd decided that he'd had enough of it. His was a short career in politics — short, successful and at the top. I suppose, if you can do that, then that's the way to go.

I think his decision to move out on his own terms showed careful thinking about his future and what he wanted to do. You can't hold that against him. The party was less than impressed for a while, because they knew he was a major selling point. But this time, Bill English, unlike in 2002, stepped up and performed exceptionally well in the election. Unfortunately, for him, the mathematics of MMP said it wasn't enough. The National Party is looking to where its coalition partner might be in the future. I think it should be with the Greens, but it would take some time to see whether the Greens would be interested. After the last election I appointed myself to reach out to a few senior people in the Green Party. Some were interested, but the majority weren't. That's a pity because I believe a National–Green coalition would be good for New Zealand.

Another way of thinking about leadership is to look at how people address serious issues or problems. Take the retirement age. Sooner or later some leader is going to have to step up and address this. The numbers over 65 are about 747,000 now, and they'll be about 1.4 million by 2040. That's the reality. You just have to face it. This is not emotional politics. We have to welcome the fact that New Zealanders are healthier and living longer and that should be something we celebrate. There is the corollary of that, of course, that we should lift the age that people are given universal pensions. That I would describe as sensible business-like leadership of a country. And, to be honest, I was disappointed that John Key ruled it out almost instantly and that Jacinda Ardern has ruled it out for her term, too.

It's disappointing because the status quo can't go on forever. National superannuation has been a political issue for years. I faced the same issue and campaigned on it in 1990, saying that we would lift the age of retirement. As I've said, it was, as far as I was concerned back then, an unwise decision by Muldoon to guarantee 80 per cent of the average ordinary wage at age 60: universal, non-means tested. To me it was obvious from the beginning that it was unaffordable long term and when I was elected PM in 1990 we moved the age of entitlement up to age 65.

The best decisions involve courage, and that was certainly the case for my team when we worked on a modern settlement process for Māori. One of the unsettling things in the United States is the movement to give reparation to the descendants of slaves. I was talking to a conservative Trump supporter the other day, a good friend. We don't mention Trump very often because that doesn't go anywhere. I mentioned something about this process and he said, 'Oh, we couldn't do that, couldn't do that.' I pointed out that we'd done something similar in New Zealand and the world hadn't stopped. We're going forward! But in its time treaty settlements were the issue that's divided the National Party and New Zealand more than anything else.

But the great news, from my perspective, is that the National Party and New Zealand were forced by my actions and those of other key members of the caucus and Cabinet to reconsider its position. Today it's not an issue in the party, except for a small minority.

I was fortunate to have Doug Graham as my treaty negotiations minister. Doug, a descendant of Highland Scots, had a natural empathy with Māori and was open to finding the sensible compromises needed to resolve such long-standing issues. I was also guided by the wise words of a friend and senior Māori leader, the late Graham Latimer, who said to me early on, 'Be certain when you're reaching a settlement to resolve one grievance for Māori that you don't create another one.' I was always mindful of that advice. I always acknowledge the courage of Tainui, who were prepared to step up and be the first settlement and lay the groundwork for our modern treaty settlement process.

The most unusual settlement agreement was with Tūhoe, which happened when John Key was prime minister and Chris Finlayson was treaty negotiations minister. The Tūhoe people had suffered greatly from early colonial policies. They had never signed the Treaty of Waitangi, because, as I used to say, 'No one was brave enough to venture into the rugged and remote Urewera to ask them.'

I wasn't involved with the Crown negotiating team, which was ably led by John Wood early on, but I was impressed with the work that John and Tāmati Kruger, the chair of Tūhoe, and others in both negotiating teams had put in to bring both sides close to an agreement. At this point Chris Finlayson invited me to join the negotiations in what was hoped would be a breakthrough meeting in gaining acceptance of a really radical new concept: that the 'land owns itself'. Under this approach it was the combined responsibility of Tūhoe and the Crown (the government) to nurture, protect and care for Te Urewera, that notably beautiful, rugged and challenging landscape. I was pleased to contribute to this visionary approach.

The beauty of that new approach was that it would bypass what could be years of negotiations on the issue of who owned Te Urewera — and remember that many Tūhoe people live in Te Urewera; it is their homeland. This new approach is a challenge to the notion that land, which endures forever, can be owned by those who don't live forever. Looked at from that perspective, what is now called ownership is really a licence to occupy and use land for a while. We pass but the land endures. I like the saying: 'You don't inherit land from your forebears, you borrow it from your successors.' That philosophy imposes a real obligation on the current generation to protect and nurture what is really only borrowed. And it's a powerful argument to protect our environment.

The Urewera settlement attracted attention across the world. A few countries, including India and Canada, have adopted similar concepts and approaches, but once again New Zealand has taken the lead. I was appointed a Crown member of the Urewera Board when it was established and I enjoy the challenge of working with fellow board members on developing this new approach.

I was also a member of a group chaired by former Māori Party co-leader Tariana Turia to explore and recommend what the government might do to assist the village of Parihaka to update its infrastructure and facilities. Again for me this was stimulating but it was also sad. The work required you to reflect on what a different New Zealand we could have had if we had adopted the philosophy of the leaders of Parihaka that there was enough for all to share. I am reflecting on whether the upheaval caused by Covid-19 will encourage people to seek a new way forward, different from conventional orthodox economics. Certainly we can't go back to old thinking.

People tend to forget that I campaigned on creating a decent society in 1990, and that certainly includes fair and equitable redress for the wrongs our colonial forebears imposed on Māori. That approach wasn't mainstream, but if you're just going to take a mainstream position, then anybody can do the job. The whole purpose of leadership is to do things differently and to produce a better end result.

Of course, yes, you want to stay in office. Yet you have to have the confidence that you can sell a sensible new argument to the majority of the people. That's really what you're arguing. That the reason that you've reached the position you're going to advance is because you've thought about it carefully, you believe it to be correct and you want to lead on it. If you have the responsibility of leadership and you've used your attention and your ability to discuss the merits of this or that proposition and it's come down on one side, then it would be almost cowardly to choose against it in favour of what's popular and mainstream. That's not leadership.

I saw this in the treaty settlements, just to go back to that for a minute, as an example of providing leadership and addressing historic wrongs. I'm really satisfied with the positions we took on such questions, which as I say were controversial at times. I don't think back and say, 'Gosh, I should have done something else.' No. You have to lead, in my view, confident that you're making the right decision and not fearful that this is going to go badly in the electorate at large or within the caucus.

I think back to that vote in favour of MMP. We were making this huge constitutional change and I said we therefore also had to move on other big constitutional issues, one of which was having our final Court of Appeal in New Zealand. It was nonsense to have law lords in London deciding matters that were totally New Zealand-centric, like treaty settlements. To me it was an absurdity. While I wasn't able to get my party to agree with that entirely, the Labour government moved on that and brought the final Court of Appeal back to New Zealand.

There were two or three other issues like this, including developing a distinctive New Zealand honours system. I asked senior Cabinet minister Philip Burdon to chair a committee to explore the options for a unique New Zealand system, which is what we have now. I raised a much bigger issue when I put forward the suggestion that New Zealand move at all due speed to become a republic within the Commonwealth, as most Commonwealth members are now. We would do that by electing our own head of state. This hasn't happened but it should. It's just quaint, to say the least, that our head of state is in London. I presume that sooner or later there will be another leader who will move on that issue. It's just about facing the reality of a changing world. Even the royal family is changing, with Prince Harry and his wife Meghan moving to Los Angeles. Change will happen.

You asked about why I don't have a knighthood. I was offered one but declined. I think I was the first to do so, but Helen Clark followed me. Helen had moved to abolish knighthoods and dames from our system, something I wasn't able to persuade my caucus to accept. But John Key brought them back, and I recall a little scramble as many who had missed out, as it were, from the Clark years said yes please when offered the chance to change their award. Both John Key and Bill English took them with enthusiasm. And my mate Brian Roche took it with enthusiasm — so it's nothing to do with me being Catholic, as some suggested. I just thought it wasn't New Zealand as I saw New Zealand. Others see it differently, but to me it was a relic from a distant past. I thought we'd moved beyond it. The interesting thing is, New Zealand likes to see itself as a leader on these sorts of issues, but Canada and Australia both gave up the British honours system long ago.

With Queen Elizabeth at Government House, Wellington, in November 1995 as she accepts the advice of her prime minister to sign into law the Waikato Tainui Settlement Act. The Act contained a full apology from the Crown for the false accusations it had levelled against Tainui to justify the confiscation of their lands in 1863.

Some people got excited about my talking about New Zealand becoming a republic as if I was attacking the royal family. I wasn't attacking them at all. I've probably met the Queen more times than most, including on the then royal yacht *Britannia*, where I calmly discussed the possibility of New Zealand becoming a republic but remaining in the Commonwealth. She's a truly remarkable woman. It's nothing to do with the personalities; rather it's to do with the principle of how New Zealand should be governed and should be seen to be governed, and whether it should be governed by somebody in a hereditary position, which is totally contrary to the democratic principles that New Zealand runs on.

And this comes back to leadership, too. You lead from the front, but you've got to have your arm around those who are behind, encourage them, bring them with you and be tolerant of them. This is so crucial to the success of communities or societies or whatever the group you're in. When my brother John spoke at my eightieth birthday he said I was the one who always led. That's where I'm comfortable.

It's also how you can deal with political opinion polls. When I was flying across Europe once with some journalists, a new poll had come out and I was so far behind it didn't matter. The journalists were all excited, but I wasn't. What was much more important — what *is* much more important — is the confidence you have in what you're doing and your ability to sell that to the electorate in due course. That's my philosophical position, and the interesting thing is, other than two very early leaders, Holland and Holyoake, I'm still the longest serving leader the party's had, so I suppose you could say it served me okay. Yes, my going was less smooth than John Key's, but that's life.

Commencement Day Lecture

Mumbai, India, 5 August 2003

Let me commence by telling you a snippet of New Zealand's history. Whereas the first civilisation in the Indus Valley occurred around 2500 BC, the first settlement of New Zealand, by people from the Pacific, didn't happen until about 4500 years later. Despite that very large gap, New Zealand and India have important shared history in that at one time we were both British colonies and that explains our deep links with Britain, our shared membership of the Commonwealth and our shared love of cricket.

What is less well known is that we have a shared history of passive resistance against British colonial rule. In the 1870s and 1880s, in the district where I grew up, a remarkable form of passive resistance took place. The indigenous Māori who had been dispossessed of their land, as a gesture of protest began to quietly plough their former land. When the first ploughmen were arrested, others came and calmly continued ploughing. Hundreds were arrested and none offered resistance.

Soon the colonial government had had enough, and on 5 November 1881, 1500 heavily armed troops, with another 1000 in reserve, set out to overcome the remarkable settlement where these so-called savages lived. The troops marched through the pre-dawn hours to gain a measure of surprise in what they expected to be a fierce battle against ferocious warriors. Instead of the expected fierce resistance they were met by children singing, and a complete refusal by the warriors to engage in battle. A remarkable man, the charismatic prophet Te Whiti o Rongomai, led the people of this village of Parihaka. Instead of battle, he suggested something quite remarkable: he offered to sit down and discuss how his people and the newly arrived Europeans might share the use of the land the Europeans so coveted.

Such an approach was beyond the intellectual framework of the then military and government leaders, as it still is in most countries, so instead of dialogue Te Whiti was arrested and eventually a special law was passed to enable the government to hold Te Whiti and some of his followers indefinitely without trial.

Before this law was passed some members of Parliament asked that Te Whiti be allowed to address Parliament from the bar of the House. This, too, was refused. The British/colonial justice system in New Zealand at that time didn't stretch to hearing both sides of the case if that was inconvenient. Perhaps the real reason was that those in authority feared that this good and charismatic man might have persuaded the Parliament to adopt a new approach to the interface between the two peoples then in New Zealand.

Te Whiti's fame grew while he was in gaol, and his term was relatively short. He was locked up for another period in 1886–87. Te Whiti o Rongomai died in 1907, a man of peace and protest to the end. The inscription on his monument at his home village, Parihaka, reads: 'He was a man who did great deeds in suppressing evil so that peace may reign as a means of salvation to all people on earth.' Almost 100 years after the death of Te Whiti, peace sadly doesn't reign on earth, and how we share the resources of the world and how we live and work with others of different faiths and cultures still challenges people of all nations.

By almost every conceivable measure, size, location, history, lifestyle and outlook, New Zealand and India are very different countries. India is a vast and complex country and, that being so, quoting averages does less than justice to many aspects of life in India. The differences are many but we are united by the universality of our needs and we are bound by our shared humanity and our shared global home. The issue of how we share the resources and wealth of the world is the underlining theme of my remarks.

My starting proposition is that the current distribution of the world's wealth, with 80 per cent of the wealth going to just 16 per cent of the world's population, with the remaining 84 per cent of the population having to survive on 20 per cent of the wealth, is simply unsustainable. I have no hesitation in nominating this as the biggest issue facing the world today and it cannot be resolved without sustained and intensive international cooperation. Two other related issues will also demand the close attention of national and international policy-makers.

The first of these is the rapid ageing of people in the developed world. The latest population projections of the United Nations (UN) show that fertility rates in the developed world have fallen from low to unsustainable. The developed world's birthrate is now 1.4 births per woman, significantly below the replacement rate of 2.1. Birthrates have also fallen dramatically in the developing world, from a rate of 6.0 in the 1960s down to 2.9 and falling. A recent UN conference on ageing noted that by 2050 seniors would outnumber children for the first time in human history. Linked to the issues of poverty and ageing will be the legal and illegal movement of large numbers of people in all regions of the world.

The world's changing demography poses huge challenges but great possibilities if the world is prepared to take a more open, liberal approach to immigration. Looking at all the big issues this is arguably the most emotive, but when we reflect on the virtual free movement of citizens through the many countries that make up the European Union progress is not impossible.

Freeing up immigration would benefit those who wish to move, and also the countries with ageing populations who will very shortly need more immigrants to work, pay taxes and provide the services the elderly will require.

Such a move would also be significant in achieving a better sharing of the world's resources. The question is, can leaders persuade their citizens to overcome their distrust and, yes, fear of people and cultures they know little of? On the experience of the EU the answer is at least a partial yes.

This is a potentially explosive mix of issues. Coupled with terrorism, they are of a complexity the likes of which the world has never been called upon to deal with before. There are no simple off-the-shelf solutions; rather they are issues of such a scale and magnitude that they have to be approached over many years and on many fronts, again at both national and international level.

I bring to my remarks on the necessity of more and deeper reform in national and international policy my experience as a senior government minister with at various times responsibility for labour and employment policy, agriculture, fisheries, immigration and policies affecting our indigenous Māori people. I was prime minister for seven years from 1990 to 1997, during which time New Zealand carried forward wide-ranging reform in many areas.

I followed that with a term as New Zealand's ambassador to Washington, 1998–2002. I now chair a number of boards in both the public and private sector and I maintain my interest in global agricultural, food and development issues through my chairmanship of the International Advisory Board of the St Louis-based World Agricultural Forum.

Perhaps most importantly, I am the son of Irish farm workers who migrated to New Zealand in 1930, I grew up on a small farm and I am pleased to say I am still farming today — the New Zealand way without subsidies. Drawing on that background, I decided my remarks would be directed at a first principles approach on the need for further reform, especially in trade policy, rather than a detailed analysis of any particular aspect of India or any other country, but I will draw some comparisons to illustrate a point.

We gather at a time of great uncertainty with tensions high everywhere. Lurking in the background is the fear or threat of terrorism, which we are reminded of every time we go through an airport. The war on Iraq has not produced a clean swift answer to anything, but it has got rid of the tyrant Saddam Hussein.

The world watches nervously as the US and other major economies teeter on the brink of deflation. The technology-driven stock market bubble burst at the end of 2000 and the resulting downturn continued through 2001 and 2002. This slowed world growth and the World Trade Organization (WTO) reported in April of this year that growth in 2003 would be less than 3 per cent, following only 2.5 per cent in 2002. In 2001, trade volumes actually declined for the first time in 20 years.

In these uncertain times the calls for freedom and liberty grow louder, but to give substance to these calls we must put in place the building block of liberty, which is economic freedom. Economic freedom is a dream, not a reality, for countless millions. To make it a reality we need to take definite and determined steps to open up opportunities for rich and poor countries alike.

These circumstances demand that world leaders pick up and run with the one big global agenda option that would guarantee a return to forward momentum in the world economy, and that is the Doha Development Round of trade negotiations under the WTO.

Negotiations in the WTO must address the huge distortions caused by massive subsidies, high tariff and import protection offered by most developed economies to their food and fibre producers. Last year, for example, America's 25,000 corporate cotton growers received $4 billion in subsidies, three times the total US aid to Africa. African farmers in Senegal have to overcome a 150 per cent tariff to export their peanuts to the US. The EU has a 200 per cent tariff on beef, wheat into Japan faces a 350 per cent tariff and the tariff on butter into Canada is 360 per cent. Current international trade policies have some of the poorest farmers in the world pitted in an unequal battle with the world's biggest treasuries. There is no freedom in that and it has to stop.

In putting forward the positive role more open trade can play, I do so conscious of the need to use land and water in ways that allow current generations to satisfy their needs, without jeopardising the capacity of future generations to meet theirs. Sustainability from this perspective is a resource-oriented, long-term global concept. I will also suggest why India should play a leading role in promoting trade reform. In urging reform, I recall what President Franklin Delano Roosevelt famously said when he surveyed what America confronted in the depths of the Great Depression of the 1930s, that 'the only thing we have to fear is fear itself'.

As the world surveys the magnitude of the issues we must address today, many seem paralysed by a similar fear. To meet the needs of the poor, we need leaders to replace fear with boldness, in the knowledge that boldness in policy development is a friend, not an enemy, of the poor. This is not a time for the faint-hearted, for remember the poor are poor because of yesterday's and today's policies. How can we stand still when existing policies have so clearly failed? New policies and approaches are needed to achieve the seismic shift in the international order necessary to provide hope, opportunity, food and clean water for all.

If we should fail through a lack of vision, or will, or courage to effect necessary change, and tensions continue to mount, then we can't ignore the possibility of facing the terrible destructive power of nuclear weapons that more and more countries, including India, argue they must have as some form of last desperate backstop.

How blowing the world apart would achieve anything is one of the great mysteries that is yet to be revealed to me. All I know is, that it is not an approach that either Gandhi or the prophet Te Whiti would have approved. When the winds of change swept over the world in the post-World War II era, we witnessed the emergence of many new and independent nations.

It was a time of great hope when powerful commitments were given to usher in more equitable policies and so enable the citizens of the new nations to achieve both their potential and their ambitions.

Nowhere were these hopes felt with greater passion than here in India. Prime Minister Nehru's speech at the moment of independence on midnight, 14 August 1947, captured this ambition as he set out his vision and hope for an India independent and free.

His words still resonate with conviction and passion for us today, when he said: 'A moment comes, which comes but rarely in history, when we step out from the old to the new; when an age ends; and when the soul of a nation, long suppressed, finds utterance.' He went on to remind his listeners that the task ahead included 'the ending of poverty and ignorance and disease and inequality of opportunity'.

India has come a long way since 1947, but I am sure that Nehru would not be happy that so much he had hoped for is still but a distant hope for many. How would he, as a man of letters, view the fact that India's literacy rate is still less than 60 per cent, with girls and women, through deliberate policy, having a much lower rate of literacy than men? What would his thoughts be when he looked across at your neighbour, China, and observed that they had achieved a literacy rate of 81 per cent, and a GDP per capita of approximately twice that of

India? I am sure he would be saddened that so many of his people, for whom he had such hope, have been left in poverty because of failed policies. I share that sadness.

Many new nations, having been exploited to varying degrees by their former colonial masters who lived in distant lands, sought to distance themselves from the world and adopt inward-looking, protectionist trade and economic policies. In so doing they compounded their problems and delayed their development. The work of Harvard scholars Jeffrey Sachs and Andrew Warner showed that between 1970 and 1990 developing countries open to world trade grew six times faster than those which were in effect closed.

The new nations were not alone in this approach. Liberal countries like New Zealand also had what now seems an unbelievable range of controls and licensing systems. Protection was provided for nearly all manufacturing businesses through import controls and high tariffs. I am pleased to say they are now virtually all gone.

Leaders of that era saw the world through a mindset that distrusted the market. They were attracted instead to the allure of planning and regulatory structures which they believed would help them manage and meddle their way to a more equitable world.

That has, or is, changing, but the change needs to go further and faster, and today's generation of leaders need to give policy expression to the knowledge that subsidies, support and protection for one group or nation are always at the expense of another group or nation.

It is tempting to blame global policies and institutions for failures. But my experience and observation convince me that the core building blocks for a country's success lie in two primary areas: the design and correct implementation of domestic policies, and the control of corruption. The then government of India clearly reached a similar conclusion when they introduced far-reaching reform from 1991 onwards, to overcome policy failure in many areas. That breakthrough in policy has paid huge dividends for millions but clearly much more must be done. You don't need any visitor to tell you of the raw poverty that is the constant companion of millions of your fellow countrymen and -women.

According to the Food and Agricultural Organization of the United Nations over 225 million Indians remain chronically undernourished and the United Nations Development Programme reports that over half of all Indian pre-schoolers suffer from malnutrition. The human cost of past failure is tragically very high. Fortunately there are many more positive signs as well. Since the reforms of the 1990s the Indian economy has posted a strong 5 to 7 per cent average growth rate. India also has a world-class software industry, and a very large entrepreneurial middle class approaching the same number as the total population of the United States.

India is still missing out on what is crucial to maintaining strong sustained economic growth and that is foreign direct investment. Foreign investment only goes to where it is wanted and then only to the country and investment proposal where the competitive environment is most attractive. Here the news is not good for India.

The *World Competitiveness Yearbook 2002*, in overall rankings, lists India at 42 out of 49, with Brazil at 35 and China at 31. New Zealand was nineteenth and the USA was first. On the three important categories, government efficiency, business efficiency and infrastructure, India ranked at 44, 40 and 47, again out of 49. Brazil ranked at 38, 33 and 37, with China at 30, 43 and 35. The figures speak for themselves, and in this crucial area for a developing economy I want to encourage policy-makers in India to continue to press forward. Good results will follow the implementation of good policy.

The optimist in me says that as these failings relate primarily to domestic policy, then solutions can be brought through quickly, when there is a will to do so. In an integrated world the global community has an interest in these issues because failed policies in many countries have directed focus onto the new issue that I discussed earlier and that is the movement of people worldwide. To escape poverty and/or oppression a growing number of people either legally or illegally seek to find a new home somewhere else.

Despite the growing economic integration of the world, and the free flow of capital, countries are very sensitive about migration and illegal immigrants. That sensitivity has multiplied many times since recent terrorist attacks. The September 11 2001 attacks on America changed the world. The terms terrorism and security now dominate world dialogue. The fact that such an attack was successfully mounted against the most powerful country in world history sent a particular chill around the world, but in fairness such an attack against any major capital would have sent similar shock waves to people and governments everywhere.

Since September 11 the world has spent endless hours and spent countless billions of dollars on the issue of terrorism and security and will continue to do so. This is all understandable, but it is an illusion to believe that real long-term security can be achieved by erecting barriers, however constructed, or by investing billions in ever more sophisticated military hardware.

Forty-plus years ago similar issues were addressed, on a cold January day in 1961, at the height of the Cold War, when President John F. Kennedy delivered his memorable inaugural speech, where he said: 'To those people in the huts and villages of half the globe struggling to break the bonds of mass misery, we pledge our best efforts to help them help themselves, for whatever period is required — not because the communists may be doing it, not because we seek their votes, but because it is right.' He then went on to give another powerful reason for such help by saying, 'If a free society cannot help the many who are poor, it cannot save the few who are rich.' That speech, while restating the bedrock ethical reason for action, also added the pragmatic, but important, proposition, that to save the rich we need to help the poor. The developed world needs to reflect anew on that observation.

President Kennedy's remarks were delivered at the beginning of the Green Revolution when, with the development of new hybrid grains, better knowledge and more fertiliser, the world was able to help poor countries achieve vast increases in food production and prevent widespread starvation.

In meeting today's food needs there are important scientific, environmental and ethical questions that will figure prominently in any debate. There are the enduring questions concerning the ownership and use of land and water, now with an increased focus on water. To that we must add the application and use of new technologies including genetic modification, and the other controversial environmental topic, global warming. And then there is politics.

It is accepted by most, if not all, that global warming is real and has clear implications for agriculture and the environment. The Kyoto Protocol drawn up in 1997 has been controversial in many quarters, yet as at May 2003, 84 parties have signed and 109 parties have ratified or acceded to it. When Russia ratifies, as expected, the protocol will come into force. The US, the world's biggest polluter, is a notable exception from the Kyoto agreement. That's somewhat surprising, given the possible implications for the US from global warming as identified by the US Environmental Protection Agency (EPA) on their website.

The EPA notes that sea levels are rising more rapidly along the US coast than worldwide. Studies by the EPA and others estimate that sea levels could rise by one foot (30 centimetres) by 2050, but that could occur as early as 2025. Needless to say, a one-foot rise in sea levels would gravely threaten communities and homes in many coastal regions.

Looking out to the next century, the EPA reports that an incredible two-foot rise in sea levels is most likely, but an unbelievable four-foot rise is possible. Let us hope that never happens, but the question of global warming is an issue that the world can't walk away from, as there is new and stronger evidence that most of the warming over the last 50 years is attributable to human activities . . . It is self-evident that developing countries faced with high levels of poverty will need to use all available tools, including new technologies, where they can be safely used.

New Zealand established a royal commission two years ago to study genetic modification. The commission received extensive submissions from interested parties at home and abroad. After many months of study it produced a comprehensive report with the key finding that 'It would be unwise to turn our backs on the potential advantages on offer, but we should proceed carefully, minimising and managing risks.' The major theme of the report is about 'preserving opportunities'.

There are many views and it's good to have them aired. On balance my chief concern is slightly different; it is that the major corporations, who do much of the research, will not put enough effort into developing solutions for the very small and very poor farmers who grow for their own use or for sale to others equally poor. To meet world food requirements, much of which comes from small farms, will require government agencies to address this issue. The development of GM crops in the future won't by itself solve all problems, just as the Green Revolution didn't solve every food problem in the 1960s and

1970s but it did enable untold millions to avoid starvation.

The September 11 attacks showed with stark clarity that terrorists can strike anywhere. Of equal importance it showed that much greater attention needs to be paid to the circumstances that give rise to such hatred. We know with absolute certainty that no child comes into the world hating anyone: children have to be taught to hate. The counsel of despair is to build higher walls to protect the few. The counsel of wisdom is to tear down the walls that deny millions the necessities of life and access to basic justice.

Some difficult political choices have to be made. If countries make decisions based only on what satisfies short-term selfish political interests, then by what logic do they expect those who grow up in circumstances where thousands die daily from preventable disease and starvation, and where there is little or no hope, to be interested in, much less share, our horror of random acts of terrorism? They live with their version of terror every day of their lives.

This is not only an issue for rich countries. There are many living in privilege and wilfully ignoring injustices in the developing world as well. President Kennedy's words apply equally to both. 'If we cannot help the many who are poor, we cannot save the few who are rich.' Those words now have a more prophetic if haunting ring. My position is unambiguous, and that is that the terrorist networks must go. But that of itself is not enough. It's a way point, not an end point. The world needs to replace terrorist networks with a network of countries, leaders and individuals who will work with passion and commitment to usher in a more just world, and so replace despair with hope.

I now invite you to think about issues like agriculture and the environment in this broader context. The issue is not only about producing food in a responsible manner, it is also about the commerce of food distribution, about minimising disadvantage by having a more open and ethical world trading system. Free nations are rightly prepared to take great risks, to put the lives of their citizens on the line and collectively spend billions of dollars to combat terrorism.

To confront your enemies on the field of battle requires undoubted courage, but dare I suggest that for governments to confront their friends and political supporters with the stark message that they intend to cut tariffs, reduce subsidies and open up markets so as to encourage the more rational use of land and to improve market opportunities for the world's poorest farmers, requires an extra special brand of courage and moral leadership.

I know that such leadership is demanding but it's absolutely essential that the world address these issues, because as we speak one billion people live in absolute poverty and 24,000 die every day from hunger. It is a myth to claim, as some do, that such poverty is due to globalisation. Rather the reverse is true, the poor are poor not because of too much globalisation, but because of too little. Too many barriers still remain that prevent workers in poorer countries benefiting from their labours.

Pope John Paul II put it this way: 'The struggle against hunger and malnutrition requires that all countries should come together to adopt new and binding regulations responding to the changed demands of trade and international exchange and not to the interests of a small number of countries.'

That was the hope in 1948, when in the shadow of World War II, world leaders decided to establish the World Bank, the International Monetary Fund and the General Agreement on Tariffs and Trade (GATT), now the WTO. These three organisations were established to assist growth and development and global economic security.

Consistent with that ambition, export subsidies for non-agricultural goods were prohibited under GATT, but unfortunately were permitted in agriculture. The result is predictable. Global tariff on industrial products is about 4 per cent and import quotas for such products have essentially been abolished.

In agriculture it's a different picture. Global tariffs average 62 per cent and much of agricultural trade is still distorted by subsidies and quotas to the detriment of developing economies. In response, Brazil, Thailand and Australia joined forces last month in requesting a WTO panel to examine Europe's sugar subsidies. The Australian minister noted that Europe spent more than $A12.7 billion on price support and export subsidies to maintain its position as the world's largest sugar exporter. This type of policy makes it hard or impossible for farmers in poor countries to sell their produce to rich countries. A ruling against Europe could force the European Union to dump the sugar subsidies altogether, which would be a huge benefit to many developing economies.

It has always amazed me that there is often strong protest and action against the WTO in poorer countries. Rather than protest, there should be support as developing countries need the WTO and a rules-based system of international trade. They need an independent international process to which aggrieved countries can submit a case in the knowledge that the facts of the case will be fairly examined and a finding issued. Without such a process, small and developing countries are in the impossible position of competing against wealthy countries with huge treasuries. A more open approach to trade won't solve every problem, but it would help to make the process of international economic integration work better for more people.

I know from New Zealand's experience that developed countries can successfully and profitably farm without subsidies, quotas or tariff protection. I also know that this poses a particular challenge for a number of developed countries whose farmers receive an increasing proportion of their net income from farming their governments rather than from farming their land.

It need not be like that. Leaders have the opportunity in the Doha Development Round of the WTO to make a change. For that to happen member countries will need to leave historic baggage behind and be willing to compromise if all are to benefit from further trade liberalisation. Multilateral trade negotiations under the WTO are the only way to design a smooth transition to more market-determined farming practices.

There are so many compelling reasons to change. The OECD confirms that agricultural support now costs taxpayers and consumers over $US350 billion worldwide. To put that staggering amount into context, it is twice the value of the total farm exports from the entire developing world.

To further support the case as to why the developing world should be the loudest voice calling for trade reform, I draw your attention to a recent World Bank study which estimates that complete global trade liberalisation by 2015 could, by that time, increase global income by $US2800 billion, with the majority of that increased income going to developing countries. That, it stated, would lift a further 320 million people out of poverty. If the nations of the world would unite for this common cause that is the staggering prize the world could win. There are many complications to overcome but liberalising world trade in agriculture is the key to unlocking the door to faster global development. Over 60 per cent of the workforce in most developing countries, including India, is engaged in agriculture or food production.

Of course it's not only subsidies and international trade policy which cause harm. Governments in some countries have much to answer for. There are corrupt regimes that waste billions of dollars, mismanaged economies that waste billions of dollars, and in many developing countries the military's share of GNP is many times greater than the total amount of overseas development assistance they receive. Yes, it's a shameful waste in desperately poor countries, but to me that's not an excuse for not reforming trade policy. That corrupt governments exist doesn't invalidate the need for others to commit to usher in, not a perfect world, but a more equitable world, where people at least have food and clean water.

Like-minded countries face two great battles in the twenty-first century: the battle to control terrorism and the battle to substantially reduce poverty. As I have indicated, they are not unconnected, and they are both battles the international community needs to win.

Let me talk about the way ahead and the role that India could play. The world needs a strong, committed voice to articulate the requirements of developing countries and so focus the negotiations on the changes needed. India, as the world's largest democracy, has the opportunity, if not the obligation, to take up that leadership role and so help guide the participants to a just and sustainable outcome. If I might borrow from Nehru, and repeat his words, 'A moment comes, which comes but rarely in history, when we step out from the old into the new.'

For India to carry out this historic role, India's government must look at all of its domestic policies to make them consistent with the ambition to usher in for the first time ever international trade policies that treat rich and poor countries with equal fairness. I do not wish to over simplify an endlessly complex problem, but the cause is more than worthy of our commitment and passion. We can't turn away, and so a more forceful stand is called for. In this campaign we don't bring the force of arms, but the force of justice for those who have for too long been left with scraps from rich countries' tables.

Negotiators can draw strength from the knowledge that, if they succeed, they will be reaching out and improving the lives of millions in huts and villages across the globe. The sober reality is that, away from the limelight, the posturing and positioning, millions of lives rest on achieving a breakthrough in this round of world trade talks.

It is not impossible, and there are some signs of progress. The EU, which provides the largest amount of subsidies to its farmers, agreed at the end of June 2003 to implement change on a scale that would not have been contemplated as recently as two years ago. What is proposed is to decouple payments from production targets, so as not to create excess production in one area, which distorts the market for other producers.

We don't know whether it was moral or financial pressure that finally brought about this change, but we do know that change comes from applying pressure at the right time. Recall how loud and powerful were the united voices that correctly called for the abolition of the apartheid policies of white-ruled South Africa and how they succeeded in helping to usher in a new era.

It is time for the leaders of developing countries to again unite and call for the realignment of global trade to facilitate the more equitable sharing of the world's wealth. We should use this moment, when the world is focused on terrorism and its underlying causes, to tear down protectionist walls between the developed and developing world, and instead of walls build bridges through trade between different cultures, ethnic groups and those of different religious convictions.

'The world is large,' wrote Irish poet John Boyle O'Reilly, 'when its weary leagues two loving hearts divide,/But the world is small, when your enemy is loose on the other side.' Today no nation, large or small, can be indifferent to the fate of others, near or far. Modern economics, weapons and communications have made us realise, more than ever before, that we are one human family and this shared planet is our home. Our shared home cries out for leaders who have the courage to see past today's inequities to a different tomorrow, the emotional commitment to dream of that different world and the passion to motivate others to do what needs to be done to make it happen.

Let me conclude with the observation that India, as the world's largest democracy, with its huge home market, an entrepreneurial middle class, plus a commercial history that stretches back through time, is positioned to play a pivotal role in deciding how the world safely negotiates the complex range of issues that it now confronts.

Armageddon

I said it, and I meant it: no long conversations about policy matters. As fascinating as they may still be to political historians, I didn't see much point in going over most of the old twists and turns once again. Except for one: nukes.

Because of the subject's national importance, obviously, and because of the political price tag New Zealand's lonely decision to go nuclear free carried, but also because of what it possibly said about Jim himself. How had he come to attach himself to an issue identified with the political left and sort of make it his own in terms of the repositioning of his party? Why did it mean so much to him anyway?

On a conversational note, what also fascinated me is how this all played out with a man who otherwise would fancy himself as a classic utilitarian, somebody who (more or less) spent a political career believing in the greatest good for the greatest number.

Nuclear weaponry has been in the political air for as long as Jim Bolger has been politically alive. The detonation of nuclear devices over Japan in 1945 still rates as one of his earliest international political memories. He was around at the beginning of the country's stormy history of anti-nuclear diplomacy, which more or less dates from the independence of colonial Algeria in the 1960s.

That last event spurred the country's former French colonial power to move its offshore nuclear activity from Africa to the South Pacific. In 1973, a year after Jim entered Parliament, Norman Kirk sent two frigates to protest against French nuclear testing at Moruroa Atoll, 1250 kilometres south-east of Tahiti, which became the site of France's atmospheric nuclear testing. Its name also became a byword for New Zealand's role as what Kirk called 'the conscience of the world'.

Kirk's move put the wind in the sails of the anti-nuclear movement and what would become the country's signature foreign policy. That fight against nuclear weapons still provides the most sustained example of New Zealand's ambiguous approach to international affairs, which both stresses the country's 'independent' bona fides on the one hand, while on the other pulling out all the stops to avoid ruffling feathers on the trade front. Much later Jim would keenly feel the tension between these two positions during his years as a diplomat.

Nine years on, it was the United States on the political radar. The nuclear-powered USS *Truxtun* made its third visit to New Zealand in May 1982, arriving in Wellington on a magically still night — in full view of the Beehive.

Later, in 1995, now in his second term as prime minister, Jim effectively squared off against the President of France, Jacques Chirac, after Chirac announced his country would conduct a final series of eight nuclear weapon tests in the South Pacific.

The rift between the United States and New Zealand on nuclear issues had a long history — long before I became prime minister. It had been a big debate in the lead-up to the 1984 and 1987 elections. It was certainly still alive when I led the party to victory in 1990. But of course it goes back further than any of that, too, to at least when former prime minister Norman Kirk dispatched the two navy frigates, HMNZS *Otago* and *Canterbury*, into the test area, with a Cabinet minister on board, in protest against French nuclear testing at Moruroa. In fact, it goes back even further than that, back to New Zealand in 1959 voting in favour of a UN General Assembly resolution condemning French nuclear testing in the Sahara, a position we took with Canada, but against the United States, the United Kingdom and France. So that awareness has been there almost from the time we even had nuclear weapons in the world. For many leaders at various times, then, in the broadest context, it has been a dominant foreign policy issue.

By the time I became opposition leader, David Lange had announced we were leaving, or had been suspended from, the ANZUS agreement. The climate between New Zealand and the United States was chilly, even as the issue was still hot. America clearly didn't like our anti-nuclear stance. New Zealand obviously was strongly supportive of it. But the National Party I led was somewhat sceptical, or at any rate by no means unanimous, that this was the right thing to do. For them, what mattered was the intent of the security agreement signed in 1951 between New Zealand, the United States and Australia to have a common defence approach.

Then there was the matter of political feelings on the American side. They were totally committed to the nuclear deterrent, as indeed were the other members of the UN Security Council. So we had to work our way — well, actually, more like *find* a way — forward. As PM, my task was to use the forums and mechanisms by which I could break down some of the antagonism that emanated from Washington, and some of these other capitals, including our nearest in Australia, who, I have to say, were also angry with us.

I did this in a variety of ways. The first that bore fruit took place when I spoke for the first time at the United Nations in 1991. A huge number of leaders were down to speak, and thanks to excellent staff work, I spoke before President George Herbert Walker Bush. Which of course meant I had a full house, something few speakers at the UN ever get to enjoy. I'd met President Bush before; we knew each other. When we had lunch after the speeches with the secretary-general, Javier Pérez de Cuéllar, I pointed out to President Bush that he was fortunate that I had spoken first to bring the crowd in.

That evening, the Americans held a reception for the leaders at one of the big New York hotels. It had been agreed through our various staff that President Bush and I would meet afterwards. A room was set aside and Terence O'Brien, our ambassador to the United Nations, came with me. President Bush brought with him Brent Scowcroft, who was his national security advisor, and who had also been his advisor on the first Iraq War. We had an open and frank discussion and at the far end of this quite large room, Joan and Barbara Bush were chatting about other stuff.

It was as simple as that, really, just a willingness of two leaders to talk about what had become a difficult issue. Bush took a clear position. But he also told me that the US would pretty soon announce they were taking nuclear weapons off surface vessels. Which was the beginning of the rollback of an aggressive posture on nuclear weapons by the United States and I saw that as a big step forward.

The elder Bush was a good person to work with, calm, reasonable and deliberate. I remember in 1984 we spent a couple of hours together standing in a bitterly cold and snowy Red Square, in Moscow, for the funeral of President Yuri Andropov. We couldn't understand a word of what was being said about the recently departed, so we had a lot of time to talk about the world in general while the others were eulogising the late Soviet leader and his 15-month rule. And there had been other times, too. So we had a background of talking.

Up until then, I think, some of the, shall we say, *flamboyant* language that was adopted on both sides at senior level hadn't been helpful. People were saying stuff that may have sounded good to their own supporters but normally didn't advance the journey towards a resolution of the problem. Then again, the politics of the day also can't be ignored. I mean, if you look back you can see the time when the Labour leadership were actually only opposed to nuclear weapons, and not to nuclear propulsion, which, of course, is an entirely different concept — in fact, in today's world, you could say a very clean concept in terms of pollution. But the eventual legislation that was passed by the then Labour government included a ban on both nuclear propulsion and nuclear weapons.

In my own discussions with President Bush, I said that I thought that the question of propulsion had to be checked and that we would put in an expert panel under Justice Edward Somers, with all the relevant expertise to see whether nuclear propulsion was or wasn't safe. That commission, which comprised the High Court judge and three eminent persons, spent 12 months on what was an impressively detailed work, the nub of which was that propulsion posed no environmental risk or public safety risk to justify continuing the ban on the nuclear-propelled ships.

But the politics of the day had moved on. So while logic would have said that we should move on and allow nuclear-propelled vessels into New Zealand, something had changed in the public mind: propulsion and weapons had become one and the same. People weren't even interested in discussing the Somers report. It's funny. As far as I know, it's still recognised as a logical and thorough and respectable report, but there just wasn't any receptive mood for it.

In the meantime, there was still the question of the National Party coming to its own position of acceptance. This happened slowly. Some say that the naysayers had their minds changed by their families, and I can certainly think of one or two for whom that was true. For me, it was different. I've always found nuclear weapons abhorrent. I mean, intuitively, in my gut, the idea that you would drop something that totally and utterly indiscriminately destroyed innocent people, men, women and children, I've found incomprehensible. I well remember as a boy when the two bombs were dropped on Japan in August 1945. I remember the excitement that some people felt, but I also remember thinking about other nine-year-olds like me who would have been in Hiroshima and Nagasaki on those days. And so, 40 years on, I didn't have any great difficulty accepting the argument. Our world would be a much happier place if there were no nuclear weapons.

Still, it was an argument that had to be made in our caucus. It didn't really deter me, though. I do think that if something is the correct course to follow I will find a way of following it. But the caucus themselves were also listening carefully, not only to their families but their constituencies, because these were the days of the old system in which everybody had a constituency they were ultimately answerable to. And the mindset of people in those constituencies — of New Zealanders in general — had moved on, all the more so because of the somewhat arrogant stance taken by the United States and other international actors.

What followed next, of course, was the case New Zealand brought against nukes to the UN to the International Court of Justice. At issue specifically was the legality of the use, or threatened use, of nuclear weapons. The ICJ came down quite clearly against the threat or the use of nuclear weapons, which, when you think about, doesn't take that much intelligence to work out.

A year on, however, the issue was back on the table because of French nuclear testing in the Pacific. I remember having a discussion about it in 1995 with President Chirac. We had been standing together on the fringes of a United Nations fiftieth anniversary meeting in which he had been rehearsing familiar arguments and bluster about the 'safety' of France's testing. I said, 'Well, if it's safe, then test off the coast of France. Why come all the way down to the Pacific? You know if this is a totally safe operation then there's nothing to fear about doing it off the coast of France.'

There was silence. Unsurprisingly. There was no logical explanation or argument to be made. Let's go back to the 1985 French attack on the *Rainbow Warrior*, the Greenpeace vessel berthed peacefully in Auckland in their supposed ally's port. And yet the French sent down saboteurs and blew it up, killing one of the activists on board. Thanks to some extraordinary detective work, we were able to apprehend two of the saboteurs and they were put through the due legal process in New Zealand, resulting in both receiving stiff prison sentences.

Later, as we know, the French heavied the New Zealand government, forcing them to release those prisoners back to France, supposedly to do time in the Pacific on one of the French islands, but that didn't last terribly long, either. So there you had New Zealand being brutally put upon by a large power called France. It was terrible. It was an emotional time for New Zealand.

New Zealand's national relationship with the issue went back a long way. And it just grew and grew. For me, the interesting thing was always how it grew in New Zealand but didn't develop in other countries, at least not in the same way. Well, maybe in some small countries but not their larger counterparts. That's the sad history of humankind, right? The side with the better weapons tends to win, and you simply have to possess big weapons because somebody else might attack you. Whereas I think smaller countries look much more realistically at the impact on the people concerned. They're more aware of the environment, too, which is something we were really thinking about in New Zealand because of the various frightening scenarios of nuclear winters, which were a regular topic of discussion and debate some years back.

People sometimes ask why New Zealand alone of those smaller nations took a stand. I think it comes back to the settler ethos of the country that we were talking about earlier in respect of those who settled the country, including our original settlers, the Māori. They've all been people who had the courage to take the risks associated with going a long way to an unknown land in the south-west Pacific. I've always felt that the gene pool of New Zealanders has had within it an extra dose of courage to take quite bold, some might say irrational, steps but we've been prepared to reach further and go further. That and the fact that our scientific community was presenting quite scary data about what such a nuclear winter would look like and the specific impact on countries like ours.

So all this, as I say, was not a rarefied debate in isolation between politicians and political parties, or even a discussion only involving the elite. This was a debate that reached right down into the crevices of New Zealand, which is precisely the place the National Party has always believed it best reflects.

I guess the rock bottom was reached after the bombing of the *Rainbow Warrior* and the subsequent legal processes that event put in motion. And that really continued with New Zealand's opposition to the testing in the Pacific. But slowly and surely the weight of public and the world's opinion was against first atmospheric testing, then against nuclear testing full stop. So suddenly, or so it seemed, the world community started to move to ban nuclear testing. And slowly France also came to the conclusion that they had to stop and halt their nuclear testing.

This all came into sharp focus at the Commonwealth Heads of Government Meeting in 1995, which I hosted in Auckland and Queenstown. It was a remarkable gathering in many respects. For one thing, Nelson Mandela had been elected president of South Africa, which meant that South Africa was coming back into the Commonwealth fold for the first time since its withdrawal in 1961. I had already enjoyed the good fortune of meeting Mandela in Harare, in Zimbabwe, quite soon after he had been released after 27 years in captivity. We had breakfast together. I remember being impressed by him on several fronts, but most of all because he didn't say a bitter word about anybody. That was amazing. Here you had somebody who

It was Jim's good fortune to be among the first outsiders to meet Nelson Mandela after he was released from prison in 1990.

had been locked up for 27 years for . . . well, for what? Asking for civil rights for his people. And yet, even so, no bitterness. Extraordinary.

In 1995 Mandela was also helpful on another front. We were at the leaders' retreat in Queenstown when the message came through that Nigeria had executed nine environmental activists, including the writer and human rights activist Ken Saro-Wiwa, all of whom said they had been framed on account of their activism against the impact of multinational oil companies on the local environment. They were killed despite worldwide pleas for clemency. I said, that as the chair of the Commonwealth Heads of Government, my view was that if we were prepared to stand by and do nothing when one of our members did that, then I wasn't sure I wanted New Zealand in the Commonwealth. Mandela took the point, and together we were able to get the Commonwealth to suspend the membership of Nigeria. And I thought that was exactly the right thing to do.

But the *other* big issue there was the resolution on the non-nuclear South Pacific. This was passed by the leaders, but British prime minister John Major abstained, which was unsurprising given his country's earlier dismay over New Zealand's policy. I knew John well and I knew he wasn't happy with the resolution, but I think he fully understood the views of everybody at Queenstown. Being calm was his style; he always seemed to take things in a thoughtful, considered manner, without shouting or histrionics, yet he was also clear that on this we were on different sides of the argument, Britain being on the side of the nuclear deterrence argument. At the same time, though, I think he wisely knew that he wasn't going to convince the Commonwealth on the matter of the nuclear issue and while he put forward the British view — and I suppose the view of the nuclear powers in general — it was in somewhat of a forlorn effort to change everybody else's mind.

I had my first engagement on nukes with President Bill Clinton in 1993. I think that's where the *real* step forward was made in the rapprochement between New Zealand and the United States. It was the first APEC leaders' meeting, which was held off Washington state on Blake Island, in Puget Sound, the birthplace of local Native American Chief Si'ahl, after whom Seattle is named. I arrived there just two days after I knew I had enough votes to form a government after the 1993 election.

As we went across from the mainland to the island on the ferry I noticed that Clinton had moved to the stern of the vessel and was leaning over the rail, just taking things in. He was on his own. I went over, introduced myself and then said that I thought there were some issues it would be good to chat about, including New Zealand's position on nuclear weapons and also the fact New Zealand had not had a prime ministerial visit to Washington for about 10 years.

We chatted for a while and Clinton said that he had not focused on the issue and had just carried forward the position he inherited, but when he was back in Washington he would bring it up for review. And yes, I should come and visit him in Washington. And Clinton did review the policy and I did visit him at the White House for a very comprehensive programme. In diplomatic terms all the stops were pulled out to ensure a successful series of meetings. And even in 2020, while we still have disagreement on the merits of nuclear weapons, we have re-established normal relationship between two friendly countries that have tremendous shared histories.

And why not? I remember pointing out to him that New Zealand had supported the first American-led effort to push Saddam Hussein's forces out of Kuwait, so it was hard to explain to New Zealanders that we could work together on causes like that and yet still not be able to have what I termed a normal relationship on other issues. Actually, it was ridiculous. I think Clinton understood that. So from there we started to rebuild a normal relationship, but I've always considered that was one of the turning points, to just have a frank but friendly discussion away from everybody else. Just the two of us. I think he was open-minded about it because it was a policy he had inherited, and he accepted the basic proposition that sensible countries should be able to resolve these things in a sensible way.

New Zealand must continue to provide a leadership voice in the non-proliferation, and the eventual elimination, of nuclear weapons. We have more nuclear states now than we had some years back, and we know that North Korea is one of the nations seeking nuclear weapons. It looked like they might change that path but nothing is certain with North Korea. We know that India and Pakistan have nuclear weapons. The only country I know that has given up nuclear weapons is South Africa, plus three former Soviet republics, Ukraine, Belarus and Kazakhstan, which inherited nuclear weapons when they broke from the old Soviet Union.

But the leadership, the real leadership, still has to come from the nations in the nuclear club. It is utter madness for countries like the United States and Russia to have thousands of nuclear weapons. There's no scenario that anybody can create in which all those weapons could ever be used. We did have a period not that long ago in world politics where nuclear weapons were being destroyed. That seems to have slowed down or stopped altogether. That debate needs to be energised again. And it does require leadership from the big powers. New Zealand can play a role. We can keep pushing the issue forward in international forums, like the United Nations.

But still, the big guys really have to play a role. I mean the British and the French, who have been nuclear powers for a long time, even if they are small nuclear powers compared with Russia and the United

States. But imagine the power of the symbolism and the reality if those two countries gave up their nuclear weapons. Where are they going to use them, and against whom? I don't know whether nuclear powers ever sit down and ask themselves in what circumstances would we ever use these weapons. Is there any way we can use 3000 nuclear weapons? And the answer is, of course there isn't. So, you either remain silent or you speak. I always say you have to speak if something is wrong. If you don't, who else is going to do it?

Yes, you're right about there being a certain irony in that the 1984 election was called allegedly against Marilyn Waring's position on the nuclear issue, and yet it fell to me some years later to reverse the party's historical position. Indeed. But going back to something we've chatted about, I believe that if there's a problem then the status quo never works as a solution. Because that's my logic: if a solution isn't needed, then there isn't a problem. Equally, I have to say, and I argued about this as a Young Farmer debater, the horror of nuclear weapons was never something I needed convincing about.

I was intuitively on the other side of that argument. But I was also aware where the National Party's instincts were. They were instincts based on fellowship in a world community. They were instincts based on America being seen as pivotal to New Zealand not being invaded by Japan in World War II. While this seemed quite a long time before, there were many within the broader National organisation as well as in the party caucus who had vivid memories of this and the Japanese move across the Pacific. I respected that viewpoint. We chatted about this the other week. It wasn't ancient history for them. We weren't talking about the Romans. We were talking something that happened in their lifetimes.

And that's where history catches up. Australia brought its troops home from Europe to protect Australia when Japan entered the war, but New Zealand didn't. We left our troops in North Africa and Europe and relied on America to protect us. Many in the National Party, for understandable reasons of history, wanted to hold on to the old order of ANZUS, even if that meant we needed to accept the concept of the nuclear deterrent. So yes, that's what I mean, there was that historic connection, and the strength of that connection was why Rob Muldoon and the majority of the National Party didn't want to take an irreversible step to isolate ourselves from the ANZUS treaty.

Now, it's all history. People like Marilyn and many others persuaded us, ultimately, that the future was not in nuclear weapons. They were right, and what they were saying was in keeping with what New Zealand as a nation had been getting at for 50 years. Yes, a divide did open up. But over time we managed to put it to one side and keep going forward, which happened to a large extent during my time as prime minister but also, finally, and more completely, when I was New Zealand's ambassador in Washington. The then chief of US defense not only came to my farewell but stayed till the end. A difficult period was behind us.

Washington

‘No way are you going to get me to provide commentary on the Monica Lewinsky affair,’ Jim said firmly. Well, he would say that, wouldn’t he? He made the remark to me two decades ago in Washington. In 2020 he’s more than pleased to look back not only on the years of the Lewinsky saga but also his entire time spent in the American capital.

Ah, Washington. A diplomatic city of Southern efficiency and Northern charm, as John F. Kennedy once archly put it. It’s a hard cultural road to hoe for any visiting New Zealander. I know because I once lived there for a couple of years. It also meant I got to know the New Zealand embassy, which I used to pass some days with my girlfriend as we headed over to the shops and restaurants located on nearby Wisconsin Avenue.

The New Zealand mission is tucked away in a quiet little cul-de-sac called Observatory Circle. It’s an inauspicious-looking building, a bit dark on the inside, too. But inside, it’s energetic enough in terms of activity, and probably more so during the four years Jim and Joan made their home there until 2002.

The media don’t really get diplomacy, which tends to be

caricatured as endless cocktail parties and dinner functions. Little could be further from the reality. Like the seas across which our exports travel, New Zealand's economic bounty has always risen or fallen on the quality of our trading activity. The value of that bounty depends a lot on the quality of the country's negotiators. This is a reality that goes back to our first shipment of frozen meat dispatched on the *Dunedin* in 1882. The success of that voyage is widely seen as having lifted the colony out of its first major economic depression.

That inaugural voyage from Port Chalmers to London also paved the way for the trade in frozen meat and dairy products that became the cornerstone of a New Zealand economy which, for many decades, meant our country operated as Britain's farm. Today the New Zealand export sector sustains more than half a million New Zealand jobs. Or, put another way, one in every four New Zealanders in work today depends on exports for their livelihoods, and the growth of areas like export education and tourism — when it's safe to have tourists come here again — aren't likely to change the fundamentals, which are still to be found on the farms and in the forests. Trade is also an important driver of productivity, employment and incomes. We know, for instance, that a New Zealand worker's productivity is 36 per cent greater if they are in an exporting rather than a non-exporting business.

In this sense, Jim's appointment as the New Zealand ambassador to Washington was almost less notable for his having been a former prime minister than for his having been a farmer. Given how important the agriculture sector is to the country, it's striking how few of our envoys have such a pedigree.

Trade opportunities do not simply create themselves.

Especially not for a country such as New Zealand, which produces much more in the way of goods (which always travel at the mercy of tariffs) than services (which generally do not). Something else that isn't often appreciated by journalists — and I'm not sure I understood this when I interviewed Jim in 1998 in his (on the day I popped in) rather gloomy office — is that these deals are always diplomatically negotiated, a skill requiring a certain artistry and good timing, a lack of rigid thinking and, perhaps least considered, good psychological and conversational skills. Those qualities probably also help to explain a little about Jim's deep-seated disagreement with the policies of President Donald Trump.

Our conversation started on the slightly theoretical level of David Hackett Fischer's hefty book, *Fairness and Freedom: A History of Two Open Societies: New Zealand and the United States*. In this book, Fischer, a Brandeis University professor, meditates long on the question of the foundational values of New Zealand and the United States. The American settlers, he posits, were primarily concerned with escaping harassment, hence their enthusiasm for counting liberty before all other political values. The Antipodeans, on the other hand, were more interested in ducking the class systems of the old world, and so plumped for egalitarianism, or fairness, as a guiding virtue, not least in the nation's political arrangements. Well, that's his comparative theory anyway. Our former man in Washington has a few of those, too.

Yes, it's an interesting book. I think Fischer ended up coming down strongly on the side of fairness. Of course, I think that's a really powerful word we've lost sight of, and losing it is what's causing many of the issues, including gross inequality, in the world today. Although I don't think that gross 'inequality' had anything to do with 9/11 — which would be an interesting point on which to start discussing my time in Washington — but it has an awful lot to do with much of the unease and unrest across the developed as well as the developing world. Some would say the scale of unfairness was just as bad in the sixteenth or seventeenth centuries. I read somewhere that in 2017 the world's billionaires added 20 per cent to their wealth, which was US$1.5 trillion, while kids are going to school hungry.

So, Washington. The case of the British ambassador Sir Kim Darroch is an interesting place to begin. Darroch had to resign his position in 2019 because of leaked cables showing that he said rude things about Mr Trump. What was equally interesting in that whole circus is how the then foreign minister, Boris Johnson, wouldn't back his ambassador but then rang up afterwards to tell him he was a fine fellow. I mean, really, how do the two largest nations of the English-speaking world, the US and the UK, manage to have two almost identical ideologues and egocentric personalities as their leaders? I just don't understand it.

Of course, and here I speak with a bit of experience, diplomats do have a requirement to be . . . well, diplomatic. Yet they also have a responsibility, which is the whole purpose or a substantive part of the purpose, to report with some accuracy on what is happening and what is likely to happen that might affect the home country. What Darroch was apparently doing in the leaked cables was giving a frank assessment of what he, watching up close, had determined to be the characteristics of Donald Trump. I have to say, I thought he was accurate in that characterisation.

Why it became an issue, of course, was because somebody thought it was good media copy and leaked it. Then Donald Trump does his normal thing and throws his toys out of the cot and screams and shouts and says, 'This is a terrible stupid man', and so on and so on. But from the other side, an ambassador has to be able to send honest and frank advice back to his or her home government. After all, if they're not going to do that, why have them? It costs a lot of money to have diplomats in a foreign country, especially in a place like Washington, where I worked during some of the time of Bill Clinton and then George W. Bush.

Why did I take up the post? Well, it wasn't a complex choice from my perspective at all. It was perhaps a little more complex from Joan's. I'd always had an interest in American politics and I knew that the post was to become vacant reasonably soon. I was also aware that former prime ministers who remain on the backbenches or even in the country can become nuisances if they have too much spare time. So it seemed much more worthwhile to become New Zealand's representative in Washington. Joan and I both enjoyed our time in Washington and made some great friends there who we keep in contact with.

In Wellington, I told the coup plotters that I wasn't going to contest the matter. I wouldn't demand a vote: I'd leave them to their problems. I mean, I didn't think they would be very successful, which was an easy prophecy to make. I would instead post myself to Washington. Well, they agreed to it, and Jenny Shipley arranged the necessary protocols for that to happen. I went six or seven months later and I was very happy. I think it was a relief for the Shipley team that I would be out of the country and therefore wouldn't be doing what they would describe as 'a Rob Muldoon' — you know, offering comments from the sidelines. Perhaps I might have been tempted to do so, too. I'm often tempted to offer comments.

Political leadership and diplomatic leadership are different settings, but by definition they're about leadership. You either have it or you don't. For me, it was really transferring the leadership skills I'd had as prime minister and minister into this other different role working out of leafy Observatory Circle in Washington DC.

One difference between the two is that politics is largely in the public space, whereas diplomacy is more in the people space; it's all about interactions. In that sense, the skills are indeed different, but compatible. Don't forget, too, that I was not the first political figure to make the switch. Former prime minister Bill Rowling had been in Washington as ambassador. And former ministers Lance Adams-Schneider and Frank Gill went there, too, so it wasn't an unknown path. I'm sure there is a pecking order of sorts between the various embassies in Washington but if there is, it really didn't bother me because I had something most of them had never had: I had run a country. Other ambassadors had come up through the diplomatic corps or some such.

After I arrived, I changed things around a bit. I used to bring the senior staff in on a Monday morning to talk about what I saw in the week ahead that was relevant to New Zealand and to ask the others to advise me what they were doing, whether defence or trade or culture. Having a united approach was important. Here again this was similar to what I did when I was prime minister, when I would bring in the Prime Minister's Department for a Monday morning briefing before Cabinet. (I think that stopped as soon as I left as well.)

There was another plus from being a former prime minister, and that was being one of a small group of people who had had political experience as well as ambassadorial diplomatic experience. This counts for something in the capital of capitals. For me, it led to a large number of invitations to go to various places or meet with various senior people in the administration or to speak at universities, whether in Texas or California or Georgetown, which was just down the road. All pluses. And no, I didn't find them challenging to adjust to, to be honest, and at the end of the day I was working for the same master I had always had, which was New Zealand.

The two big issues were the nuclear stand-off and trade. The United States talks a big talk on free trade but is not very good at implementing it, which continues up until today as far as that goes.

I also arrived at the start of the Monica Lewinsky scandal. It certainly dominated the television channels night after night after night. You couldn't not follow it, as it were. You had to take an interest. I was hosting a dinner on the night President Clinton was going to give his presentation on television about the scandal, and it was going to be quite late so that it would be shown live on both coasts. My memory tells me he went on at about 9.30 in the evening — it might even have been 10 o'clock East Coast time. This dinner for about 20 guests included the then US secretary of labour. We got to the end of the meal and I looked at Joan and said to our guests, 'President Clinton is going to go on television in five minutes and the only television in the residence is upstairs in the library.' And they all got up to the library faster than I did. They all wanted to watch the president's statement. And of course everybody remembers his line: 'I did not have sexual relations with that woman, Miss Lewinsky.'

In the end, I met Clinton a number of times. I've met him since as well. I remember going to an event at which he was speaking where they put up the proverbial rope line for people to go up and shake hands with the president. I thought I should do it, too, because I knew I was leaving in a week or two to come back to New Zealand and I wanted to say thanks and farewell. It was funny as could be, because beside me was a mature American woman who wanted to talk to the president about a ball game. About halfway through this long dissertation — Clinton was as patient as could be and paid her full attention — she beckoned another friend to come up and join the conversation. Through all this Clinton gave no indication that he saw me there at all.

But then immediately he moved to me, his opening line was, 'Jim, tell Wellington that I will get that motion through Congress.' That motion was on nuclear disarmament, which he had not been able to have passed. He was genuinely aware of New Zealand's great disappointment over this.

I met both the Bushes a number of times. I first met George Bush Senior when he visited New Zealand as vice president in 1982, in Russia in 1984 and also at the United Nations in 1995, and various times in between. I found Barbara Bush an interesting woman. She seemed to have honest views that she was more than prepared to express. She was forthright. The Bushes and Joan and I had a mutual friend and

Jim and Joan met President Bill Clinton and First Lady Hillary Clinton on a number of occasions.

we'd had dinner with them at a friend's place in Texas. Bush Senior was extremely approachable. He had an enquiring mind — probably more enquiring than his son — and would ask good questions. His son, I think, would have made a perfectly competent president if it hadn't been for 9/11, which was an event so outside the mindset of 98 per cent of Americans, and that included him. It totally derailed him, leaving the hardliners in the Republican Party — people like Donald Rumsfeld, Dick Cheney and co. — to basically take over the running of the policy of America. And the rest, as we know, is history.

On the other hand, you could just say that 9/11 was outside the mindset of 98 per cent of diplomats, too. I remember the morning it happened. I was at a breakfast in downtown Washington with a finance group who were briefing us on the economy. I'm not sure whether there were other diplomats there, but there almost certainly were. We had only just finished the briefing and were standing around chatting, when one of the people there who had some sort of electronic device — this was before texting — said that a plane had hit the World Trade Center. It didn't cause immediate anxiety. Small planes had hit it before.

I went down to my car and when I got in, the driver, Brendan Chetham, a big lad from Northland, said to me, 'A second tower has been hit.' I replied, 'Can't be an accident.' So we drove back to the New Zealand embassy, which was just a few minutes away, and I went to my office to hear the television newsreader say that a *third* plane had hit the Pentagon, which meant that it had probably flown above where the embassy is to get there. A fourth plane was understood to be heading to Washington.

I was thinking to myself, well, where's the fourth one going to go? The White House? The Capitol? And if it doesn't hit one of those, there's the vice president's residence on the other side of the road from where we are and the British residence on the other side of us. A few minutes later, though, we heard about a plane that had crashed in Pennsylvania, and that was the fourth plane.

Obviously everybody remained glued to the box to see what was happening and to see, as happened shortly afterwards, the collapse of the Twin Towers. I had recently been to the top of the World Trade Center on an earlier visit to New York, and to see them both just crumble was nightmarish. To see people jumping out of windows . . . it was terrible. I felt incredible dismay. But also, lingering at the back of my mind, was the big question of *why*.

And then, later, when it turned out that most of the Al-Qaeda hijackers were Saudi nationals, the question only felt deeper, because Saudi Arabia is supposedly the closest friend that America has in the Middle East. And how did these people manage to take over four planes? Not one but four planes, virtually simultaneously, and fly them into the Twin Towers and the Pentagon and wherever the fourth was bound? I don't feel those questions have ever really been answered. Yes, there were explanations of how these young men had got in and trained as pilots and so forth and so on, but . . .

It was interesting for me how quickly passengers on the fourth plane learnt to fight back. Once they knew what was going to happen because the hijackers, foolishly I suppose from their perspective, allowed people to ring home, which enabled them to understand what was happening. They reported for duty, as it were, and courageously fought back. Hence what happened in the skies above Pennsylvania.

In the wake of the attacks, every plane was grounded in the United States except for the US Air Force and Saudi planes that flew across America to pick up Saudi citizens and ferry them out. Which I find incredible, just incredible, and it was also incredible that America's response was not to attack Saudi Arabia but rather Iraq. Just inexplicable. I can still see the chairman of the Joint Chiefs of Staff, General Colin Powell, on television pointing out all the supposed nuclear sites in Iraq to justify the attack, but sadly little of it was true, which he admitted later. Again, this has really not received the condemnation or coverage that it should have. Yes, Saddam Hussein needed to go, but the whole Iraq war was built on a lie, and thousands of lives were lost, far, far more than were lost in the Twin Towers attack.

Diplomatically, though, as all this was happening, everything was in a state of chaos. The president vanished from sight. The most visible leader quickly became the New York mayor, Rudy Giuliani, who these days is better known as one of President Trump's right-hand men. But on the day, there he was walking the streets of New York to offer support and encouragement to the citizens. It was as if he had become the temporary president because no one knew where the real one was, which I think turned out to be Louisiana. That was surprising to me. I know that there would have been security concerns but I would have thought that the country's leader would be visible to offer support to a shocked and shattered country. He would only regain his voice three days later when he visited New York with a loudhailer.

What happened in America was a loss of innocence. The American public had relied on the infallibility of their military to protect them in all circumstances from conflicts that were far away. That was the standard belief. American greatness would always protect the homeland. Yet here they had absolutely incontrovertible evidence that that wasn't so.

The show of patriotism was instant. I said to someone on the day, 'What we should do now is get a line of American flags because there'll be a big demand for American flags after this.' Which there was. Those flags appeared everywhere. I don't have a memory of

above Lunch with Rod Stewart and Rachel Hunter at the Trentham races.

left A roadside sign in Northland, photographed by a Bolger staff member.

hoisting one outside our mission but I noticed that a lot of them were made in China, and I always thought there was a certain irony in that.

The outburst of 'We will show we're proud Americans' was understandable but in the early days, or even weeks — in my view, anyway — there was no rational discussion about *why* this happened. You could have a discussion on why it wasn't prevented but no one seemed to be venturing into why these people had decided they would attack America. Why would Saudis, who were allegedly friends of America, want to attack America in such a spectacular way? That discussion was never really engaged in.

I think this was probably influenced by America's constantly moving and shifting Middle Eastern policies. I remember talking to a senior American about how, when Russia was invading Afghanistan, the Afghans were allies of the United States and they were arranging for military material to get to the Mujahideen to help them fight off the Russians. But once that was over, they became enemies of America again. That constant churn, that turmoil, in Middle Eastern politics still continues.

At the time I think I had my head around some of this better than most, in the sense that I've always felt I could understand the sense of oppression that some groups have had, and that includes Māori in New Zealand, because of my Irish ancestry.

We're a race that has been oppressed for centuries by the English. So somewhere in our gene pool we can empathise with the plight of others. I always felt, for example, that the terrible tragedy of the Highland clearances in Scotland also gave those of Scottish or Highland descent an empathy with Māori. I always felt that my good friend Duncan MacIntyre, who I worked with early on on treaty issues, had that same sense, coming as he did from people who experienced the Highland clearances — the forced eviction of tenants of the Scottish Highlands and western islands, mostly in the period between 1750 and the mid-nineteenth century. If your ancestors have been through the trauma of forced evictions from your traditional homeland then you empathise when you see others suffering in a similar manner.

But people don't always learn these lessons, and often they're not taught well. Look at Iran, the world's pariah, or more correctly, America's pariah, at the moment. Back in 1951, in a free and democratic election, Mohammad Mossadegh was elected prime minister. But he upset the status quo in that he, understandably in my view, wanted some of the oil wealth from wells on Iranian land for Iran. At that time it was all going to what was called Anglo-Iranian Oil, but is now called BP, and none to the Iranian people. He couldn't get a deal with Anglo-Iranian Oil, so he nationalised the oil industry. This was when the Labour government in Britain was also nationalising some elements of British industry. This wasn't a way out-in-space idea. But both the Americans and the British thought what Mossadegh was doing was *outrageous* so they mounted two coups to remove him, and when they were successful in their second attempt, in 1953, they locked him up under house arrest for life and brought back the Shah. And he acquiesced to the continued exploitation of Iran by Western countries and companies. So entrenched in the minds of some in the Middle East is this deep sense of unfairness that they have been subjected to over decades, if not centuries.

In his 2003 book *All the Shah's Men, New York Times* senior writer Stephen Kinzer says 'it's not far-fetched' to draw a line from the overthrow of Mossadegh 'through to the Shah's repressive regime and the Islamic Revolution to the fireballs that engulfed the World

Trade Center in New York'. Well, history has a long reach. The attack understandably dominated world news and for a short time that autumn, I became the voice of New Zealand in the media. Everyone was talking with me. It was as if it was my responsibility to give an on-site view of what was happening. Personally, I always thought that one of the better responses was when President Bush visited the mosque that was quite close to our embassy, and which Joan and I used to walk past frequently on the way into central Washington. At that mosque President Bush stated that he did not attribute the attack to Islam — to the religion, to the faith. It was done by individuals, who yes, were Muslims, but he was not attributing it to Islam. Which I thought was an important distinction.

About a month after, maybe less, the New Zealand and Australian consul generals in New York arranged for an interfaith service to be held in the closest church to Ground Zero. It happened to be a Catholic church, and it also happened to have an Australian priest. The service was attended by a few hundred people and when I spoke as part of my remarks I read a letter from Prime Minister Helen Clark, expressing New Zealand's deepest sympathy to all devastated by the attack. I was in constant contact with Helen Clark during that time.

To some extent 9/11 was similar to the mosque attacks in Christchurch. Shattered innocence. In both countries, there was an outreach to the various faith groups to bring people together again. We had quite a lot of that. There was a big service in Washington's Episcopal Cathedral, which I attended. Again, that outreach was part and parcel of the immediate response to the tragedy, a clear human response to both events, which involved ordinary citizens rejecting the barbarity of what happened and embracing those who were hurt.

What was different, though, was that in New Zealand we moved to ban certain categories of weapons and we've put in more surveillance here and there. America did the surveillance bit in spades, but they didn't ban weapons. And it changed the perception of America's position in the world. Obviously, and correctly, the attack attracted huge support of the US because Americans were the victims, though the actual victims came from many countries. But it was American sovereignty that had been violated. The unspoken reaction was, 'If this can happen to America, what could happen back home?' If the military might of America can be breached, then what protection do smaller countries have? I suppose the enduring message is that determined — some would use the word 'fanatical' — people can breach almost any barrier to achieve their goal, especially if their lives are on the line as well.

Then there was the invasion of Iraq, and all that horror there — a dark chapter not only in American history, but also in world history, because it precipitated still more events and had an impact on everyday things like the tightening of security in airports around the world, including New Zealand, that we now have to endure. What did it all signify? Some say it spurred a lot of the terrorism we have seen around the world in recent years, but violence has long been inflicted by small groups on larger groups — by small groups who feel they're victimised — all through history. One thing 9/11 did spark was a great boon for the arms industry. Do you remember President Eisenhower's last speech from the White House? Here was a man who knew the horrors of war from close personal experience. He said calmly, in his last message to the American people, that they must be aware of the power of the 'military–industrial complex'. Today we should still heed his words carefully. Because wars are terrible for the individuals and the societies concerned but great business for the military–industrial complex. Mr Trump has boasted about the big arms sales he's made to Saudi Arabia.

So many lies. I mean, if you draw the comparison now between Clinton and Bush, the two presidents during my term as ambassador in Washington, you would say that they complied with presidential norms, if I can put it that way. They had their different views and expressed things differently, but they were presidential. But President Trump is non-presidential, and makes a feature of being rude and boorish to any group he doesn't like. Running a country by Twitter is so extraordinary — we've lost our sense of surprise.

Telling lies no longer attracts attention. They are so common. That is the fatal legacy of President Trump. He has destroyed standards in a manner that would've been considered inconceivable under Clinton or Bush. Clinton had his issues, but nothing on the scale of Trump, who, according to the *Washington Post*, had told more than 16,000 documented lies by the beginning of 2020. Journalists are starting to comment now, that no matter how outrageous what he says is, it ends up on the back page the next day. It is so common. People have become accustomed to the lies and don't push back. The most amazing thing in America at the moment is that these staunch God-fearing Republicans just allow him to continue.

What New Zealanders don't realise is how far to the right the Republicans are of the National Party and how much right of the Labour Party the Democrats are. I've said many times that New Zealanders, in the main, would be Democrats. But look, I got on very well in America. I enjoyed my time there. But the legacy of slavery and subjugation is still part of the American story and still influences some of the Americans' decisions, and that is of course entirely different to New Zealand. While there's no doubt that Māori were treated poorly, and their assets and land were stolen, there was never the master–servant relationship of the American slave movement. Remember, President Johnson had to overcome an 84-day filibuster in the Senate to pass his Civil Rights Act in the early 1960s — not that long ago, when you think about it.

I was happy enough to be coming home when we left. I think by that point I had seen through bits of the glitter and glamour. We'd had a good team of professionals working with us on New Zealand's interests, which was mainly re-establishing a sensible security understanding after the ANZUS bust-up and looking to advance New Zealand's trade interests, which was a constant battle.

And we met and made quite a number of friends there, some of whom we still have regular contact with. It was great — as long as you didn't talk about guns. Talking about guns, it doesn't matter which side of the fence you're on, you're wasting your time. It's one of those interesting delusions: the idea of guns and liberty. But it's not liberty if 40,000 people die from them each year. No other country kills as many people with guns. If a terrorist kills two people, it's a national emergency. Around 40,000 Americans get killed each year by guns. And that's liberty? Fairness or freedom? You tell me.

Anzac Lecture

Georgetown University, United States, April 2006

Thank you for honouring me with this invitation to deliver the annual Anzac Day Lecture. I am conscious of both the outstanding speakers who have delivered this address before me, and the unique environment that is Georgetown University and the role it has and continues to play in the life of these United States of America.

Every Anzac address I deliver makes me think again, and each time more deeply, of the events that lead to war and the terrible impact of war on people, the innocent and guilty alike. And on each occasion I seek to extract something new that might help us in some way to avoid the tragedy of war.

The person whose vision led to the founding of this university was Father, later Bishop, John Carroll, who was a cousin of the Charles Carroll who co-signed the Declaration of Independence in 1776. The construction of this university was started 10 years later in 1789 and the first student, one William Gaston, arrived in 1791 and eventually went on to serve in the US Congress.

The tragedy of war visited this university with the Civil War and it's reported that in 1861 many students 'left the university in anticipation of war' and given that the university was in the old South it is perhaps not surprising, if to me somewhat sad, that the great majority joined the ranks of the Confederate army. The memories and scars of that conflict still linger in the dark hours before dawn.

Given that the central issue of the Civil War was slavery, it is notable that 10 years after the end of that war a new president took the helm at Georgetown, one Father Patrick Healy, whose father was an Irish immigrant and whose mother, Mary, was a slave woman. Georgetown can rightly feel proud that their Father Healy was the first descendant of an African American to gain a PhD and the first to lead a previously white university.

Now if we move forward a short 50 years we witness the start of another civil war, although it is usually known as World War I. It was a civil war in the sense that the leading participants were known to one another and the royal families in many of the countries were related either through family or marriage.

There are many lessons that should be learnt and relearnt from the Gallipoli and Dardanelles campaign. But first I want to step back and look at the build-up to this civil war. As is known, on 28 June 1914 a young Serbian nationalist assassinated Archduke Francis Ferdinand, the heir to the throne of the Austro-Hungarian Empire.

The British historian Martin Gilbert, in his biography, *Churchill: A Life*, relates how the British Cabinet was meeting on 25 July 1914, discussing how to draw an acceptable boundary between Northern Ireland and the Republic of Ireland, when a note was handed in with the Austrian ultimatum to Serbia. Churchill clearly thought the demands were impossible and persuaded Prime Minister Asquith of the wisdom to move some naval capability to be better positioned to defend the English coastline.

Churchill's feeling at what was happening is best captured in a letter he sent three days later to his wife, Clementine. 'Everything tends towards catastrophe and collapse', he said, and went on to observe that 'I cannot feel that we in this island are in any serious degree responsible for the wave of madness which has swept the mind of Christendom. No one can measure the consequences. I wondered whether those stupid Kings and Emperors could not assemble together and revivify kingship by saving the nations from hell but we all drift on in a kind of dull cataleptic trance. As if it was somebody else's operation.'

With obvious changes you don't have to think for long to see similarities to the world we live in today. And that is the really scary part because, despite the clarity of Churchill's view, personalities and politics became seemingly more important than working together for solutions.

And so the drama was played out. First Germany declared war on Russia, then issued an ultimatum to Belgium. Britain was bound by the Anglo–Belgian treaty of 1839 to protect Belgium and in turn then issued an ultimatum to Germany to stop the invasion in 24 hours and to maintain Belgium neutrality. The British ultimatum went unanswered and Britain and Germany were at war.

At the far side of the world Australian and New Zealand leaders and citizens alike watched anxiously as Europe imploded, little knowing that this was the fateful beginning of the Anzac story.

As the year turned from 1914 to 1915 the thought of opening a new front by landing on the Gallipoli Peninsula and forcing open the Dardanelles was gaining support. But, as seemed inevitable, internal wrangling as to the best approach delayed action and ultimately led to failure. There was debate as to whether a big naval effort by itself would be enough. To this end it was proposed that the newest British battleship, the *Queen Elizabeth*, whose huge 15-inch guns had yet to be fired, along with a large naval force, would surely destroy the forts defending the Dardanelles and then it was all straightforward to Constantinople.

Various senior British military commanders had undisguised contempt for the Turkish fighting capability. Kitchener, according to Gilbert in Churchill's biography, offered the view that no troops at all would be needed because once it was clear that the forts at the Dardanelles were being silenced, the Turkish garrison on the peninsula would flee to Asia, along with the garrison at Constantinople

. . . Perhaps it was intended as the first version of shock and awe.

The attempt to force the Dardanelles with a naval force failed and a number of battleships were destroyed by mines and no further serious attempt seemed to have been made.

Eventually it was agreed that troops were needed and agreement was reached that the 30,000 Australian and New Zealand troops en route to Egypt should be redirected to Gallipoli to join up with a force of British troops to take the peninsula.

What we should also focus on, in this era of globalisation, is that the countries that went to war were close trading partners. John Ralston Saul points out in his new book that Germany had been the leading customer of Russia, Norway, Holland, Belgium, Switzerland, Italy and Austria–Hungary; the second best of Britain, Sweden and Denmark; the third best of France; and the primary supplier to Russia, Norway, Sweden, Denmark, Holland, Switzerland, Italy, Austria–Hungary, Romania and Bulgaria, as well as the second largest to Britain, Belgium and France.

As we know, neither these investments nor trade stopped these countries from slaughtering each other in an unprecedented way for four years. An unbelievable tragedy.

Waikanae

Some Irish sage once said that a thought, a sword and a spade should never be allowed to rust, which more or less accurately captures Jim Bolger's attitude — and there's evidence of all three on our final morning shortly before the great lockdown. Outside the dining area window, as ever, the gardens are impressively manicured. Over the fence men who have touched life at many points are playing golf. They say the spectacle of golf is like watching paint dry, but I've always thought that's unfair on paint. Yet the sleepiness of the game does provide a useful contrast to an interestingly restless conversation with someone who enjoys facts and their use.

We had been down to talk more about New Zealand's current leadership. What shape was the current administration in? How was the still tender Jacinda Ardern faring? We had chatted a lot about the past — but what about the direction in which the current prime minister, in particular, was helping to navigate the country Jim once led?

The exchange ended up being more freewheeling. So much so that, unlike our earlier talks, it seemed to make better sense to present it in a standard question-and-answer format.

On reflection, the lack of terribly much discussion about the current premier may have been fortuitous. When we started meeting in early 2019, the country's then relatively new prime minister still seemed rather lightweight. Much was waiting to be said about her lack of performance. And then everything changed.

First, in the wake of the Muslim massacre in Christchurch, she stepped up as the nation's mourner-in-chief. That explosion of violence showered many sparks on much dry tinder. But she handled it. Then White Island blew its volcanic top. She fronted that one well, too. Then came the 2020 pandemic — and any previous verdicts on the prime minister, in particular, would become almost entirely irrelevant as she rose or fell on the strength of her response to the zoonotic plague.

The array of challenges — here a medical emergency unfolding, there an economic meltdown looming or even the collapse of a significant part of the education or farming systems — spurred most of the country to rally around. Judgements on other aspects of Ardern's eventful first term suddenly seemed rather out of place as this young leader found herself elucidating the meaning and odds of death rather than the kind of endless social 'improvements' that would usually be her chirpy stock in trade.

The prospect of mass illness is deeply, even metaphysically, distasteful to anyone. It's distasteful because it reminds us that death is coming and might even be with us at the next tick of the clock. Yet this must be an especially difficult message to lead on for somebody who is a social democrat. Cheerful progressives like Ardern rely on medicine's best outcomes. It's their job to celebrate these things; it's also what they usually campaign for office on. But nature has its job to do, too.

Nobody better understands the broad realities of leadership, and indeed nature and age, than Jim Bolger. He turned 85 this year. But, as he likes to point out, the last prime minister of Malaysia was 10 years his senior and he's still gladiator enough. Jim also says he is optimistic about the young, and insists on this with the certainty only a father of nine can muster.

Over final cups of tea and biscuits, then, and while other retired gents carried on with their golf, we set about putting these and other matters in the world to final rights. Jim started out — surprise, surprise — on the subject of the current American administration.

There are interesting economic reports coming out of America these days. It has a trillion-dollar budget deficit that's beyond comprehension. It's under a right-wing government who, in the US, seem to be the ones that go into debt in modern times. President Reagan left a massive deficit, which George Bush the elder then inherited and increased taxes to try to move back to balance, but failed, and Bill Clinton and his team tidied up. George Bush II left a big deficit because he decided to have a war in Iraq for no stated purpose other than it was seen by some as retribution for the 9/11 attack. But that made no sense as it wasn't the Iraqis who mounted that murderous attack. Then Obama had to tidy that up. And now there's President Trump, who has ignored Republican Party commitment to balanced budgets and instead introduced and passed a budget with a trillion-dollar deficit, and all Republicans but one voted for it.

It's a contradiction. They all campaign on sound and prudent finance, but as soon as they get close to the levers of power, they spend mainly to support their friends. This is particularly so in America because money is such a dominant influence in politics, along with the influence that the mega-rich enjoy. I suggested in a speech the other day that to prevent such a development in New Zealand, the radical thing might be to prevent any of that by introducing state funding of political parties. We already give pretty substantial funding to political parties for their campaigns on television.

Maybe we should follow the Scandinavians and fund political campaigns to avoid any possibility of money buying influence. We've got some extremely wealthy people in New Zealand and they might try to influence policy outcomes. They didn't try that when I was party leader and PM but that's a long time ago. In today's rapidly evolving politics they absolutely do influence policies in the United States and some other countries.

DC: When I lived in the US 20 or so years ago, the national debt was regarded in Doomsday terms. Everybody remembers the clock in Times Square showing the debt getting ever higher.

Yes. It's dramatically bigger now and the world still hasn't ended. But the world is still struggling. I've been reading an article by some learned fellow about what will happen if zero interest rates become the new normal. We're starting to struggle with some of these concepts. If you look back, in New Zealand terms, to Roger Douglas, and those who supported him across the political spectrum, you'll recall that they believed he had found a solution in what is now known as neoliberalism. Country after country is now rejecting neoliberalism because it has been a totally divisive policy that's now hugely challenging to resolve, because all it did was hand wealth in bucketloads to the top. Something like three or five Americans now own more than the bottom 50 per cent of the population. These are obscene comparisons.

The neoliberal model didn't work, just as the communist model didn't work. The idea that everything would be controlled by some czars in the capital failed abysmally, notwithstanding that the originators had a vision for a more equitable society. The challenge has always been finding a balance between private initiative and the market, and government making sure that the extremes didn't emerge through their legislative programmes, which has to be backed by the welfare structure.

DC: Where do you see that reflected best? Scandinavia?

Yes, in anything I've read on shared prosperity in Scandinavia. You also see it in New Zealand. We haven't gone to the extremes of many other countries. I was interested recently to see a survey on people's happiness or sense of wellbeing in the modern world. It showed that the higher-taxed countries of Scandinavia were the happiest and had a greater sense of wellbeing because, presumably, they believed that their taxes were being used constructively. They accepted the imperative of a more equitable society a long time ago, perhaps because they lived on the border with Russia, and could see the disasters of that system. I've often thought that New Zealand should spend a little more time studying the Scandinavians.

The other area in which we should study them is on penal policy, because they're closing prisons and we're building more. Relatively, our prison population is enormous. 'Lock them up!' is not working. I'm pleased to see corrections minister Kelvin Davis has been talking about that and, to be fair to him, he talked about it before he got into politics as well, so hopefully we will see a change in approach.

DC: But Scandinavia has stable, largely homogeneous populations and no colonial history to speak of, no burden of defence or international leadership.

They spend far more on defence than we do. Sweden's got a big arms industry. And think where they're situated in the world. They've got the big Russian bear beside them, metaphorically speaking. But even if New Zealand's colonial history is a factor, it's still an indictment on our country that we haven't been able to escape from that legacy, even if we are in a much better space than we were 50 years ago.

If you go back to the 1930s, there were terrible rates of unemployment, and they were terrible without counting women or Māori, because it was presumed that Māori would look after each other in the pā and women were supposed to be at home. Now we've gone past both of those attitudes, but we still have a challenge with our rising prison population in which Māori are substantially overrepresented. And we have to address growing white paranoia. Here's an example of what I mean. There was a meeting over the weekend in Hungary at which Prime Minister Viktor Orbán said that the issue was about procreation, not immigration. In other words, whites should breed more and if they did then we wouldn't need immigrants. One of the participants was the former Australian prime minister Tony Abbott. Australia, you remember, had a White Australia policy until the 1960s. That legacy continues in some ways, with some in Australia today with all its racist undercurrents.

This is one of the huge challenges of the world. There's one stark reality, if anybody looks at the arithmetic, and that is that the white race isn't going to be the dominant race in the future. It'll just blend with others.

DC: Is that a good thing or a bad thing?

If you are a rabid believer that white people are superior, then it's a disastrous thing. But if you work on the presumption, as I do, that all are equal, and the colour of a person's skin is of no matter, then it's just part of the reality that we're going to face. But, still, it's one of the big divisive issues in the world today, particularly in the United States and Europe.

This concern at possible loss of identity has ironic undertones. When the European settlers came here, they had no sense that they were taking away a Māori identity that had been here for perhaps 1000 years. It was sort of, 'We're superior and we're bringing something as a gift.' And European society did bring a great deal in terms of advanced technology, new ideas in agriculture and much more. All the evidence says that white men, wherever they went, were happy to have close personal relationships with dark-skinned women. And as each day goes by we are more prepared to acknowledge the many gifts that Māori culture and history contribute to our society.

DC: Yes, but what's happening isn't just an ineluctable fact of reality. It's a fact, yes, but something is being lost when these societies can't replenish.

It's not *can't*, it's more that they *choose* not to replenish, to use your term. Take, for example, China, where they have relaxed their long-term one child policy. You might expect that the birthrate would increase. But I read recently that there were two million fewer babies born last year. It is a complex issue. Personally I'm colour blind and I don't find any of this threatening. We're mainly talking about white people being fearful of a changing society but, as you correctly point out, it's not only white people. Japan is even further along the way of having very small families and sub-replacement fertility. Japan is a wealthy society so very small families is a choice that many are making. Simple maths will tell you where that's going, yet I understand

Japan doesn't have a formal immigration policy and reports say many are somewhat resentful of the small number of immigrants who help make its society function. Without immigration, Japan and many other wealthy countries are going to have much smaller populations in the future. Even Russia has in effect put out a recent call for more immigrants.

Then if we look at the US, many Americans express unhappiness at the number of Hispanics in the country, but if you took them out of the States, the place would stop. You'd have the same problem in most of the countries of Europe if the immigrants went home. Someone said to me only yesterday, if we didn't have Filipinos working in New Zealand care facilities and rest homes they couldn't operate.

DC: What about the theological implications? Suddenly you've got traditionally majority Christian countries dealing with a religion like Islam which, in its conservative expression, isn't entirely compatible with most of our culture and history.

Yes, religious differences. History tells us they can create tensions. We talked about the Reformation and the vicious divisions that caused, some of which last till today. I guess it's inevitable that we get presented with the extremes of Islam and other religions, because the media tends to focus on the extremes within society and through societies. The overwhelming majority of Muslim people get on with their lives. They look after their families. They do the best they can. So I don't have fears that Islam is going to somehow or other destroy everything we know and cherish. Why focus on Islam? Think of Myanmar, a majority Buddhist country and how they have treated the Rohingya people. And Myanmar has Aung San Suu Kyi, a Nobel Peace Prize winner as its leader. As I said, it's a complex issue.

DC: Well, sure. But how does that square with, let's say, quite severe religious views on what women may or may not do?

Okay, but go back 200 years in the West — I'm saying the West here in a generic sense — and there were broadly similar views on the role of women. Change is happening: even the conservative state of Saudi Arabia is now letting women drive. I was at an InterAction Council conference of former leaders in Saudi Arabia some years back where young Saudi women, all Harvard- or Oxford-educated, were in attendance but not actually participating in the conference. They had no formal role in the exercise. One of them talked to Joan and bemoaned the fact they couldn't drive. Amazing. Yet the West keeps in close contact with Saudi Arabia, which supports a most extreme version of Islam, which is to say, Wahhabism. And don't forget that Saudi Arabia was the first country that Trump visited as president. Why? You tell me.

But even in our regional backyard, in, say, Brunei, for instance, there is now the death penalty for homosexuals, and I don't think we can really explain things away by noting that homosexuals were once flogged in New Zealand too. But they would be in the States right now, if some people had their way. The conservative Bible Belt in America certainly doesn't accept homosexuality as normal, to use that term.

DC: Maybe, but no one gets stoned to death.

Not yet. But think about the lynching of black Americans. This was common at one time. There is the biblical line, 'Let he who is without sin cast the first stone.' We have to look in the mirror before we cast stones. All that said, in general, we in New Zealand have certainly moved ahead in accepting the equality of people and their various orientations much more than Islam has thus far. But there are those among us who are not the moderate Christians, who would demand to be recognised as the true believers, the true carriers of the message of Christ. And they have more extreme views on what is right and what is wrong; extremes in belief aren't restricted to followers of Islam.

The only main point I'm making, David, is that we can't condemn more than two billion people because we're exposed to the extremes of some of them. Yes, there are some barbaric extremes and there's no justifying that. Also, as a practical matter, we have the world's largest Muslim nation, Indonesia, near us as our closest Asian neighbour, and we have a full relationship with them.

But what worries me is this dividing of the planet, as the hard religious right across the world tend to do, and being totally anti-Muslim. Remember that almost his first move when Donald Trump was elected was to try to ban immigrants from a number of Muslim-majority countries by executive order. The courts wisely told him he couldn't do it. Dividing countries and societies on religious grounds is not the road to a more peaceful world.

DC: Let's talk about the mosque attacks in Christchurch. You were in Azerbaijan speaking at an economic conference in Baku when you heard the news. How surprised were you?

Shocked. Horrified. It made me immediately think of what happened the week after I became prime minister, when we had the Aramoana massacre in which 14 people were shot by a lone gunman. There was the same sense of hopelessness. I visited that modest little community immediately to talk to whoever I could talk to, but even while I was doing that I knew that I couldn't reverse a single thing that had happened. In the recent case, there was a similar sense of hopelessness, even worse because we were so far away from home in Baku. Helen Clark was in Baku, too, as was Jenny Shipley. We all had a similar emotional reaction, 'How in God's name did this happen in New Zealand? What caused that?' We New Zealanders could of course attempt to excuse ourselves: the killer was an Australian who had relocated himself to New Zealand. But that didn't help at all, didn't reduce the horror of the massacre of innocent people gathered in prayer.

DC: Didn't it sort of help to know that kind of racist violence was not homegrown in this instance?

No, not at all. I accept that there are white racists in New Zealand. I think what we now are starting to perhaps grapple with more, emotionally and hopefully politically, is that there are people with extreme views on race and religion. We all know of the terrible segregation there had been in South Africa, and the terrible battles over apartheid and rugby that totally divided New Zealand back in 1981. Back then, only Hugh Templeton and I in the Muldoon Cabinet opposed the 1981 tour, on the basis that proceeding with it would be terribly divisive within New Zealand, and it was. And 1981 is not that long ago. New Zealand divided itself viciously over racial equality. There was all the justification offered that politics shouldn't enter sport, whereas in South Africa politics totally dominated sports — no black people could play for the Springboks and no black or brown people could be in the New Zealand team that travelled to South Africa. Thankfully that has now changed and the Springboks, captained by a black South African, won the last Rugby World Cup. We can take inspiration from that. Policies can and do change.

No, we can't say bad racial stereotyping won't reappear, partly because of the spread of hate and strange theories through social media outlets. We have to be aware of the possibility of white racism growing in countries like New Zealand. Coming to terms with the mosque killings was a bit like processing 9/11. When something that terrible happens, it takes quite some time to work through the full implications.

DC: Do you think we have processed what happened in Christchurch and what the implications are?

No, I don't think we have at all. I don't think we've processed it in our minds in terms of what creates that person who went in there with guns to deliberately murder innocent people. I don't think we can understand, I know I can't, how someone can get so consumed by hate that they believe that murdering innocent people is the right thing to do. Unfortunately we still see what I describe as lighter versions of that. I mean that not many people actually go out and buy guns to shoot people but their intuitive reaction to people who are of a different colour, or a different faith, is very hostile. I live in hope that we will become a society that will embrace differences.

There are around 740,000 superannuitants over the age of 65 years in New Zealand today and the majority will be dead in more or less 20 years. They are overwhelmingly white. Within two decades this huge cohort of white New Zealanders will have gone to their reward and they will be replaced in general by a much more diverse group of people. This transition is happening and will continue to happen. It's unstoppable yet I'm not sure our leaders talk enough about this huge change, and so prepare society for change.

One of the sub-themes in my various speeches now is that we must manage change better — no matter what I'm speaking about or to what audience. I think that's a crucial element. Many of the economic reforms of the 1980s and 1990s were essential, but I don't think we managed all of them well. I don't think we looked after those who were totally disrupted out of what they thought was a stable lifestyle and then it was gone.

DC: How could it have been done better?

Well, we could have spent as much time worrying about the people involved as we did about the economy involved. I don't think we did. One of the first big environmental issues I was involved with was in the middle of my electorate, the virgin Pureora Forest, in 1978. That's where I met environmentalist Stephen King. The Pureora Forest had the last of the giant tōtara left standing in New Zealand, magnificent trees, and Stephen and others were protesting against the logging. People were perched in trees to prevent them being cut down. The Muldoon government decided that we would break the contract with the company that had the rights to mill the forest, and compensate them for their loss. The then minister of forests, Jonathan Elworthy, and I went into the village of Barryville to inform the workers of the government's decision and that it meant that they soon wouldn't have jobs. We sought to explain the reasons for the government's decision but I don't think we did much for them in terms of getting new jobs.

I still think about it. What an extraordinary commitment that was, to perch yourself 20 metres up in a tree and say, 'I'm not coming down.' That was near the beginning of the big environmental movements in New Zealand. But the question is: Did we look after those forestry workers and sawmillers as well as we should have? As well as we looked after the trees? And I would think the answer is no. The workers were just victims of a change in community attitudes and government policy, a change the public wanted. But what we did do was compensate the company, because we could measure the loss. It was a large sum of money. Across the world, and in our home base here, we have to manage change better. We have to have a better sense of how people's lives can be totally destroyed by a change of government policy, or totally supported through that change so that they can move on to whatever the next occupation or opportunity they have. This is a hugely important issue going forward with the massive disruption caused by the Covid-19 lockdown.

DC: Would there be examples of governments that have handled change well?

Not that I know of, to be honest. Maybe regarding climate. The Ministry of Transport has proposed to the current government that it should ban the importation of fossil-fuel vehicles from 2035, and I would put a tick beside that, because I think that's what we have to do and by setting a date 15 years in the future we give all a chance to plan for the change.

DC: What are your impressions of Jacinda Ardern?

Let me blend two things together. We had the terrible mosque massacre. I was thousands of miles away in Baku and everything I read at that time — and I did make contact with her government; not Ardern personally, as I didn't have her number, but another senior minister, to offer support. The empathy and positivity Jacinda injected into New Zealand's response was obviously 100 per cent. In everything I've read, she said the right things, she was in the right place, she showed the right empathy to those who had been totally destroyed by the shooting. She deserves all the marks that she gets for that.

But look at climate change. You've got this staid old Ministry of Transport saying, 'This is what we should do, Prime Minister. We're your advisors on transport and you should do this.' The transition away from internal combustion engines to either electric or hydrogen power is going to be a huge issue. But it's nowhere near as big an issue as the transition we made at the beginning of the twentieth century, when we went from horses to the internal combustion engine. We've only been dealing with internal combustion engines for about 100 years. So it's all doable if you have the courage to make the commitment to move forward, all doable. But will she?

DC: How do you rate her?

She has handled two big issues, the Christchurch mosque shootings and the Covid-19 response, extremely well, but I believe that the jury is still out on how she will deal with the big environmental issues that New Zealand has to address. The other classic was her commitment to a capital gains tax. We had the establishment of a committee under Michael Cullen, the issuing of the report and then the total dismissal of the report, followed by a total reversal of her campaign position. Yet having a fairer society was front and centre of her campaign. I'm not being partisan here because National won't do it either.

DC: Maybe it's a bit like John Key and superannuation. He wouldn't touch that, would he? Too difficult.

Well, neither will she. That's the other point I was going to make. I think John Key was wrong and I think Ardern's wrong on superannuation.

Tom Scott's interpretation of Parliament and the Press Gallery's reaction to Jim's final speech in Parliament, in 1999.

We're going to approximately double the number of New Zealanders eligible for superannuation in 20 years. She and John have in effect said, 'I think we can afford double the cost.' I don't. The National Party has gone back to the Bill English position of proposing to gradually lift the age of entitlement for super to age 67.

The other big step, in my time, was to start the modern treaty settlement process. That was not popular with many in the National Party or in the wider community either, let's be honest. But with the support of a few courageous ministers we got the process started and now it's 'normal' and, what's more important, it's right. You can argue about whether it was sufficient or not sufficient, or whatever, but the breakthrough had been made and a consensus was formed. There are still people who disagree, but that becomes less relevant with every passing year.

But I didn't win them all. On RNZ this morning they were talking about Māori Language Week and how there's obviously a big uptake of learning Māori in many communities. When I was prime minister I early on asked for a report into how we could introduce the teaching of Māori in primary schools and was told, No, it's impossible, we don't have the necessary teachers. On reflection I should have pressed harder, but at the same time I was focused on rebuilding the economy we had inherited. Anyway, the great news is we are now moving towards my ambition, which was that we should all learn Māori in primary school. As I put it to one audience, not in order to become great Māori orators but to understand the language better, and to be able to pronounce it better and feel comfortable when we hear it spoken.

DC: It seems to me that Ardern's great accomplishment is that she is very adept at media performance. She's skilful, looks good, sounds good, but past that point it becomes difficult to isolate triumphs.

Does it? As I've just said, she handled the shootings skilfully, she has been up front and centre in leading the response to Covid-19. New Zealand's response to the pandemic has been up there with the best. The huge challenge now, for all countries, is how to get our respective economies back and growing and people employed once again. There are no easy answers and that's a worry for New Zealand Inc. The world is going through such a transition. For example the totally huge sums of money that have been created — we used to say printed — is a new challenge. As the money has just been created and is owed to no one, I would suggest that we explore the option of just writing most of it off. Perhaps adopt a little of the newish modern monetary theory that's being promoted by some academics at Newcastle University in Australia. Radical, yes, but New Zealanders proudly like to point out how many times we were in front of the world. If we don't do something radical we will be paying of the debt for the next 20 years.

DC: What about the rise of China?

I just read a piece in the *Irish Times* about the current position of China being approximately where it was in terms of influence and dominance before colonialism took over. China is only reclaiming its position in the world, and this will be its position, according to the *Irish Times* analysis, for the next 1000 years. That sounds a brave prediction.

I do put something of a question mark on that prediction because, going back to that population issue I talked about, China's population has already started to decline and will reduce quite substantially. That might be of assistance to China because it doesn't have enough good land and water in the same place to feed itself. But I could mount an argument that China's period at the top will not be that lengthy, and then it's likely that India will emerge in a leading position in the world community. India will soon have the world's largest population, but it's more than that. They are very engaged with the possibilities of new technology, including artificial intelligence and robotics, all of which will play a huge part in tomorrow's world. The list could go on, and none of the above can guarantee positive outcomes. Those will be determined by the quality of leadership in both countries. And in some ways it's a competition between a centrally planned economy and the world's largest democracy.

What we've also got is an unusual development in that two leading countries — the United States and the UK — are both turning inwards, both withdrawing from their traditional leadership roles in world affairs. Britain is withdrawing from Europe, Scotland will likely become independent again, North Ireland may reunite with Dublin, and I won't speculate on what Wales might do. Britain was there in a partnership with 27 other countries, and now it's withdrawn to its small island home. With President Trump, the United States is clearly withdrawing from trade policies, security policies, climate policies, etc. Can anyone believe that earlier leaders like Churchill in Britain and Franklin Roosevelt or Truman in the United States would be moving away from leadership in the world community? In fact, what those leaders did was lead on promoting policies to find cooperative approaches to big issues like trade and defence.

One of the difficult issues is that both countries are divided along partisan political lines and that's not going to change any time soon. To me it is hard to understand how both countries have arrived at this point. We can look at the leaders and blame them but that doesn't explain why people voted for them. The leaders didn't hide their political agenda. I surmise the divide reflects growing wealth inequality.

We are facing a huge period of transition from the old order to the new and, as I see it, no one in the New Zealand Parliament — let's include them all — is saying anything of substance about these issues at all. Who was it who said, 'Where there is no vision, the people perish'?

DC: It's biblical. The Book of Proverbs.

Yes. I worry about a lack of vision.

DC: On the other hand, we don't have a lot of politicians standing up to China, do we?

No, but you're focusing on old-order issues and seeing China as a threat, which I don't. China is a huge country reclaiming its place in the world. I'm talking about the massive impact caused not by guns, bombs or national boundaries, but by an invisible virus. I've just mentioned the creation of trillions of dollars to keep the world economy partly afloat and to stop millions from starving. We will require creative leaders who can see new and different solutions.

You want to stay with China. China can get very annoyed when they're criticised. But Uncle Sam can, too, as we saw with the anti-nuclear policy. All credit to David Lange and Helen Clark, who I suppose were the main drivers of it. It's a good example also of a government taking an unpopular position — it was certainly unpopular with maybe more than half the population. A few weeks ago you and I talked about the committee I set up under Justice Edward Somers to study the safety of nuclear propulsion.

DC: The one that reported it was safe as houses.

Almost. In general terms the report said it was safe, but that didn't change anything as New Zealanders had adopted a strong anti-nuclear position and weren't of a mind to revisit the issue. I thought we could have reviewed our policy on nuclear propulsion when we received the report but New Zealand's mind was made up on the issue. There was little public interest when the report was released. But the environment is a much bigger issue now so maybe a brave government might decide that the report should be lifted back out of the bag, as it were, and reviewed from an environmental perspective perhaps, to power huge container vessels. Huge container ships are a big source of pollution and we must explore all options.

The point I want to make is that if we're serious about climate change, then we have to look at how we get cleaner propulsion. There's a lot of focus on aircraft at the moment for a variety of social issues. Prince Harry and Meghan Markle were roaming around the world talking about climate change, flying in their private jet, and people were pointing out the hypocrisy of that. But nobody is spending much time talking about the vast container vessels of the world. Planes are quite difficult to run without fossil fuels, but it would be easy to convert big ships to nuclear propulsion, if everybody is satisfied that it is safe.

DC: Do you think there's political timidity in New Zealand when it comes to criticising China?

No, but frankly I haven't actually given much thought to your question. Clearly now that China is the second largest economy in the world, and playing a much bigger role on world issues, its policies and practices will get more attention. How they treat their ethnic minorities is very much open to criticism. But I don't think former colonial powers, with their histories of marginalising minorities, can say much about how China is treating its minority groups, or wanting to protect its space in the Pacific. Neither should we forget how racist earlier New Zealand policies were to early Chinese immigrants. Back then we even had a special tax on Chinese.

DC: Do you ever wish you were in a government again?

[*Laughs*] I've said to Nathan Guy, our local MP, since he's standing down, that I'll run for his seat because I've got good name recognition.

DC: You could do a Mahathir bin Mohamad, you've still got years to do that.

Years! [*laughs*] I have said that. I knew Mahathir quite well. Interesting man. He's done some things that I totally disagree with. But, totally hypothetically, I'd like to be driving New Zealand forward faster on some of the changes we have to make. We're not moving forward as quickly as we need to. We're not facing some of the difficult decisions.

DC: Like on climate change?

Yes, like climate change, superannuation and welfare policies. They all have to be addressed. On super we either need to increase the age of entitlement or go to a means-tested system, and of course the means-tested one takes us back to where we used to be. We used to get an old-age pension at 60 that was means tested and a universal pension at 65. Then Rob Muldoon took everything down to age 60 and I took it back to age 65. Perhaps it would have been wiser to have gone back to the original model and have a means-tested benefit. It's hard to justify paying a pension to billionaires. On welfare reform, perhaps we should study the merits or otherwise of a universal basic income, which is being discussed more today.

DC: Becoming a republic?

Yes. It makes no sense that our head of state is in London.

DC: New Zealand should do a Brexit?

No, but as I said earlier, New Zealand should become a republic. The only other leader who supports that is probably Helen Clark. The reason we economically survived when Britain went into the EU in the 1970s is because we woke up to the part of the world we actually live in, which wasn't Western Europe but was the south-west Pacific and Asia, and we expanded our reach into Asia and its huge populations and survived well. It took Britain ditching us to make us open our eyes and say, 'They don't want us, why don't we look elsewhere?'

It's quite interesting how habit becomes destructive over time in politics. The habit was that we sailed past populations of hundreds of millions to go to a relatively small country called the United Kingdom. It was a relatively small market and we sailed to it as far away as we could without opening our eyes earlier and saying, 'Why do we go there and not somewhere closer?'

We've seen the decline of all of Western Europe. The Viktor Orbáns can try to keep out non-Caucasians, but that will fail. I would have thought that when Angela Merkel took a million refugees into Germany, she was doing two things. One, I think she is noble in her ambition to help those who are hurt, but, two, I think she was also being a totally pragmatic leader in saying, 'We need the workers anyhow'. You could tick two boxes and that's what I think we have to do. We have to have a broader vision.

The worry is that leaders like Trump and Johnson get big rallies in front of them and shout all sorts of nonsense. President Trump has created a climate where the acceptance of lies is standard. That's an extraordinarily destructive position for a world leader. They just manufacture a story to suit their monologue, and they'll change the story the next week so that it suits a different monologue.

DC: Is that a new thing?

Yes. To the extreme it's done, yes. Before Donald Trump I recall no news channel deciding it needed a fact-checker to inform viewers of the real facts.

DC: But Clinton lied. Reagan was always being accused of being an actor.

Yeah, but Clinton lied about his sexual peccadillos, and he sort of admitted that at the end. I hosted a dinner at the residence in Washington not long after he gave his famous denial about Monica Lewinsky and there wasn't a soul in the room who believed him. But I don't think he was anywhere near the serial liar that Trump is. He just puts whatever storyline that supports the argument today and then changes it tomorrow. It's an extraordinary arrogance.

DC: Does that say something about the changing nature of politics or the changing nature of communication? We've got this media thing going now 24/7, 365 days, and there's this churn of information, opinion, defence, rebuttal going on which almost leads to this situation. Maybe Trump is a radical example of leaders being under this enormous pressure to perform, to put out, to pontificate . . .

Well, go back to Angela Merkel. I don't see her having to do that. I don't see many other leaders doing it. I think it's a particular personality, an insecure personality and a big ego.

DC: And in the case of Britain, since we're talking about that, what about the democratic argument that 17.4 million people voted for a particular proposition to leave Europe, and so the government must follow their wish?

In general terms, yes, but if the campaign is based on lies there is an argument about what checks should there be. And one check would be to have a second referendum if there is only a small margin on a very big issue like Brexit.

DC: Do you think in principle that if a prime minister is delivered a binding referendum result they must accede to it?

Yes, you try to implement it. But in this specific case there was never a referendum to say, 'We will leave without any agreement.'

DC: You led New Zealand at the time of our most famous referendum, over the introduction of a mixed member proportional voting system, MMP.

So many things come down to managing change. In the future we have to manage the change that robotic workers and artificial intelligence will impose upon societies. I don't think we're putting enough energy into thinking about that. Nobody in the last election here in New Zealand even mentioned it.

I've suggested that we should be studying how we introduce a four-day week. The 40-hour, five-day week dates back to the changes caused by the first Industrial Revolution. Back then machines changed the old order and now we're facing the same again. What frustrates me is that nobody in government or in Opposition, nobody in the Parliament, is really talking about it. It's as if, 'Well, it's not our problem.'

I find that a total dereliction of the responsibilities of leaders, and I use the plural there. I don't see Simon Bridges saying anything about it; I don't see James Shaw saying anything about it. Certainly, Winston Peters isn't saying anything about it and I don't see Jacinda Ardern saying anything about it. It's almost as if they don't know it's there. But of course they know it's there, but they don't really seem to have the mindset to grasp how they're going to deal with it. My point is that it's coming, ready or not.

DC: Maybe they're just caught up in day-to-day politics?

But leaders can't have that luxury. To succeed, leaders have to be in front of issues.

DC: Is it technology that has changed or something else?

Technology is going to drive virtually all change, but leaders have to manage that. When Joan and I were in a small modern hotel in Singapore six months ago and wanted a new towel, it wasn't a human who brought it up. Instead a robotic gentleman brought it up, a little machine about a metre high, programmed to enter the lift, get out at the right floor and go to the right room bearing a towel. This isn't some distant future or theoretical exercise dreamed up by some scientist, it's happening now, yet we don't talk about it enough. We're not prepared. There aren't any tough interviewers who are prepared to push for answers in interviews with political, business or union leaders. To succeed we must prepare now for tomorrow's world.

The world will develop a vaccine to control Covid-19, but there is no vaccine that will control the disruption that the widespread introduction of artificial intelligence will have on the world of work. There is no vaccine that will control climate change. We, New Zealand and the world, have to urgently develop policies to address these issues.

Address to the Zone Four Meeting of Local Government New Zealand

Queen Elizabeth Park, Kapiti, 28 February 2020

The biggest immediate threat in the world at the moment is the coronavirus, which was first identified in Wuhan in China. And the first big lesson that the virus has reinforced is how interconnected today's world is and so every day the virus has spread further. There are the obvious upfront personal and community health risks and associated costs. The amount is as yet unknown, but very large financial costs across the world are inevitable.

China is New Zealand's largest export market and that means New Zealand will suffer significant direct financial costs as most industry sectors will be affected. The bigger issue as the virus spreads is its impact on the world economy and whether the spread, and the measures taken to control the virus, will drive a world overburdened by debt into recession.

These costs will range from food exports through to Chinese students being unable to come to New Zealand to study. Education is our fifth largest export earner. Other costs will be related mainly to the export sector like food, timber and tourism. Tourism will be a big upfront loser, but the losses will flow on to virtually all other sectors. Collectively we can expect a virus that first appeared on the other side of the world to significantly impact our economy.

Those invested in the stock market will have watched the turmoil on markets worldwide overnight in Europe. As said earlier, all wonder whether it is a so called 'correction' or will it tip an overindebted world economy into a recession. By Tuesday many markets had lost all the gains made in 2020, and the losses have continued with the New York Dow Index suffering its biggest one-day loss.

The impact of coronavirus on the New Zealand and world economy is a reminder of how important China is to the world economy.

The International Monetary Fund has estimated that China — reflect on this — accounted for 39 per cent of global economic growth in 2019. China achieved that despite Trump's America seeking to damage the Chinese economy with the imposition of various tariff increases and a trade war. We all have a deep interest in an early end to the coronavirus emergency and an end to President Trump's trade wars.

If and when the Covid-19 virus reaches New Zealand then local government will inevitably have a role to play in seeking to limit its spread. I am sure that you are all reflecting on what role you could play or are required to play.

I have been talking about one risk that threatens the world and will take untold billions to address. The important point is that no one is suggesting nor will suggest that we can't do anything because it will cost too much. I make that point because longer term a bigger threat to the world is climate change and rising sea levels around the world, including here on the Kapiti Coast.

Talk of addressing and limiting the risk of climate change and the question of the cost of taking such actions seems to be front and centre of any discussion. Why the distinction? Easy, those in authority know that the public will demand that action be taken to protect them from the virus, but with climate change the working assumption for many is that serious action can be put off for another day.

I believe that is very wrong. Instead I agree with the young Swedish activist Greta Thunberg's message to the UN Conference on the Environment in October 2019, when she said: 'People are dying. Entire ecosystems are collapsing. We are in the beginning of a mass extinction. And all you can talk about is money.'

A powerful plea for action now. I repeat that the biggest issue of our time is climate change: extreme storms, wildfires and rising sea levels will become more frequent unless changes are made starting now. Yesterday's *Guardian* carried a lead story stating, 'Australia is heating faster than the global average and extreme heat days are on the rise. Doctors say there's clear evidence that it's killing people prematurely.' It makes sombre reading.

Let me look at some of the facts regarding climate change that support the assertion that it is the biggest issue. We all know that Antarctica is the coldest continent, yet recently it posted 18.3 degrees at the Argentina research base. The highest temperature ever recorded in Antarctica, that was until a few days later when, at a different location, a 20-degrees-plus temperature was recorded.

Something very serious is happening and I urge local and central government to include serious programmes in their forward planning to start addressing this issue. Yes, some steps are being talked about, but in my view we must urgently go past talk to action.

The world's biggest iceberg, A68, some 6000 square kilometres in size and weighing about one trillion tonnes, is about to enter the Southern Ocean and will melt, adding a huge volume of water which will, of course, lift sea levels.

Despite the scale of that, an even bigger worry is the Thwaites Glacier, also called the 'doomsday glacier' because of its size. It is roughly the size of Britain and is a huge risk in terms of global warming.

Think of this. There is enough water locked up in this glacier to lift sea levels by more than half a metre — a frightening concept. The US and UK in a joint effort are engaged in a US$50 million project, the largest and most complex scientific field programme ever in Antarctica. The goal is to try to understand why the Thwaites Glacier is changing so rapidly. There is no more important work being undertaken if you live in coastal communities anywhere.

Now let me give you a really scary figure: if all the ice covering Antarctica, Greenland and in mountain glaciers were to melt, sea levels would rise about 70 metres and the ocean would cover all coastal cities. You can relax; I don't expect that to happen, but I thought it showed how huge the issue of global warming is. The world's scientists are virtually unanimous that we, the world, are not doing enough to moderate dangerous climate change.

Many of you will have read the headline in the *Dominion Post* last month: 'Warming Oceans Warn of Looming Climate Disaster'. The article goes on to inform the reader that 'the world's oceans reached their highest temperature last year since modern records began over 60 years ago'. Further, research shows that oceans are warming at an accelerating rate. Think of this: records show that they 'have risen four and a half times faster since 1987 than from 1955 to 1986'. That's hard to ignore.

We are all familiar with the Paris Climate Accords which were agreed in 2015 with commitments to limit warming to 'well below 2 degrees Celsius'. The reason for 'well below 2 degrees Celsius' is that at 2 degrees of warming, more than a third of the world's population will be subject to repeated severe heatwaves, coral reefs will 'mostly disappear' and ice-free summers in the Arctic will become 10 times more likely.

The sombre reality is that, despite all the talk at the Paris Climate Accord, emissions have actually increased by more than 4 per cent since the Paris agreement was signed and the average concentration of carbon dioxide in the atmosphere is the highest in human history.

I have included the foregoing data to remind us of the scale of the forces of nature that will be part of our changing natural world and to encourage you to take action now so that we can achieve a smooth transition from yesterday's fossil-fuel-driven world to tomorrow's world driven by clean energy.

Governments, central and local, have, in my opinion, a responsibility to provide leadership to their people, and to guide their communities through the policy changes that New Zealand must urgently implement if we are to have a smooth transition.

I don't pretend that this will be easy. Leadership at times like this requires both a clear vision on current and coming changes and the courage to take the necessary steps now before it's too late. In terms of big decisions, I encourage you to keep in mind earlier leaders who built the huge hydro schemes that now provide the majority of New Zealand's clean electricity.

Keep in mind that unless central and local governments move now, not at some undefined fuzzy time in the future, to implement policies that will make a real difference to New Zealand's carbon emissions, then history will determine that you were too timid and moved too late. I know that you have a multitude of issues to deal with and those who want to delay action will say that New Zealand is too small to make any difference. Yes, we are small, but someone has to lead, or in New Zealand's case, aspire to be part of the leadership group of nations working to save our planet from the worse implications of climate warming.

If New Zealand and the world are not prepared to do much more to drastically curb emissions, then in my mind you have an obligation to prepare your communities for a 3 to 4-degrees-plus increase in temperature, and the associated extreme weather conditions and massive costs that will go with that failure to act. Doing little or nothing now will require that you should honestly set out the much tougher decisions that will be necessary to save lives and communities in the future.

There are no easy options in this space but the worse decision would be to put off hard decisions to another day. I am confident that the world can make the necessary changes if we stop hiding from them. Recall 100 years back, our parents and grandparents made the more dramatic shift from horses to the internal combustion engine.

Speaking of timing, the new managing director of the International Monetary Fund, Kristalina Georgieva, said at the recent Davos Economic Forum, in a wonderful turn of phrase, that 'the world of finance groggily awakens to climate change'.

The story in *Time* goes on: 'For decades banks have given fossil-fuel companies the finance to mine and drill; and meanwhile governments have provided seemingly bottomless subsidies, some $US 5 trillion annually' to similar industries. Madness — no other description is adequate.

Not seeking to be unkind, I believe that government at all levels are only now — to borrow the IMF managing director's words — 'groggily waking up to the full implications of climate change'. That's a tough call but I can only make that observation by watching, and I see little happening.

The government's key policy, which they have been talking about for the last three years, to encourage buyers to make the move to clean electric vehicles by subsidising them has, like the much touted capital gains tax to help calm the housing market and bring a sense of fairness to the tax system, been abandoned. Well, that's what the media tell us. Apparently Winston Peters didn't like the scheme so it won't proceed. I had hoped that we were all waking up to the scale of the change we will need to make, but apparently I was wrong.

I recall that famous definition of madness as continuing to do the same thing over and over again and expecting a different outcome. We must keep that definition in mind when looking at present policies. We can't just continue doing what we've done before and expect a different outcome.

So I am saying you must move. What can local and central government realistically do to achieve a significant reduction in carbon emissions? What we have to do is staring us in the face. We are overcrowded with polluting motor vehicles and as it will still be some time before we have self-drive autonomous electric vehicles we must move to change the existing fleet now.

All branches of the government, again both central and local combined, are almost certain to be the biggest buyers of fossil-fuel vehicles in New Zealand. So my policy suggestion is, starting now, for all branches of government, when replacing vehicles, to only purchase non-polluting electric, hybrid or hydrogen-powered vehicles.

A short time after that policy is implemented the government should ban the importation of second-hand cars unless they are electric, hybrid or hydrogen. There will be sufficient used vehicles coming from the government fleet transition to meet the demands of the second-hand vehicle market.

What I have set out is in rough form, but I am sure, with the necessary details filled in, it would speed up the journey from polluting fossil-fuel vehicles to a clean non-polluting fleet. Remember some cities like Paris have already banned diesel vehicles to stop pollution. Of course a nationwide network of charging stations will be required and such steps should be taken without delay. Not difficult as electric power is distributed across New Zealand.

Implement the foregoing and New Zealand will have taken the first big step to achieve a significant reduction in carbon emissions. Re. hydrogen, the minister of energy, Dr Megan Woods, is hosting an event next Tuesday, which I will attend, for a presentation by First Gas which explores the practicalities of using hydrogen as a renewable energy source in New Zealand. Also, hydrogen developer Hiringa Energy has announced a partnership with Waitomo Energy for four refuelling stations next year [2021]. All moving in the right direction.

Further, a young New Zealand start-up company, Invisible Urban, has begun operation in the US providing EV charging stations in parking facilities. An article in the *New Zealand Herald* on 21 February 2020 noted that many US states require that new parking facilities cater for EV charging.

The example given was the State of Georgia, where it is now required that new parking facilities provide that a minimum of 25 per cent of spaces are equipped for EV charging. Compare that to New Zealand's two newest malls, NorthWest, with two EV charging spaces out of 1100 spaces, and Westfield Newmarket, which opened with 2700 spaces and no EV chargers.

At present in New Zealand it's all talk but little or no action. And it's not that New Zealanders can't see the future. It is that the policy settings don't encourage innovative thinking to be actioned. Let me quote another New Zealander, Dan Ammann, a Waikato lad who graduated from the University of Waikato and went on to become president of General Motors in 2015 — some achievement — before moving on to become CEO of the self-driving start-up Cruise, owned by General Motors.

Dan Ammann has called solo drivers of petrol-powered cars 'the fundamental problem behind pollution, congestion and vehicle crashes'. Ammann is now promoting the idea that the future is 'electric self-driving vehicles purpose built for ride-sharing as the best cure for modern-day urban transportation woes'.

His vision sounds very sensible to me, if we are to stop building ever more roads to cater for ever more and bigger vehicles, but still only carrying one person. An aside, I drive a plug-in hybrid and I assure you that you can get around without difficulty.

So let me conclude by briefly returning to my main proposition, that there are many steps that central and local government can take, starting tomorrow, that are not far-fetched or radical, to significantly reduce New Zealand's carbon emissions.

The important next step is for leaders to see that different tomorrow and then to take the steps needed towards the smooth transition I spoke of to achieve a different sustainable tomorrow.

Afterword

And that was that. So many Friday mornings, dozens and dozens of conversational hours, and we were done. Along with a growing bunch of tapes and notes, I asked myself, on the final day, what I was taking with me on the drive back to the city that Jim called his political home for 35 years.

It often happens that the real theme of something only emerges clearly after a lot of initial work has been completed. What had the memorable one in this exercise been? There were the personal aspects, sure, the emphasis now and then no doubt recalled in the interests of legacy as much as a disinterested historical record. As I drove back to Wellington, and then later worked through the material during an international emergency, the idea of leadership again came to mind.

Jim likes to say that leadership is about making the unpopular decisions. Kicking against the pricks. Maybe. But leadership is also about ardently negotiating situations. The former prime minister sometimes speaks of himself as somebody who challenged the status quo. I suppose most elder statesmen with a natural eye on posterity would say something along those lines. I prefer to think of him as someone who has been adept at negotiating *with* the status quo.

Such was the theme that emerged as I started putting together the various chapters and supplemental speeches. From the son of immigrants brokering a place in the local culture, a lover of debating (which itself is a negotiation of sorts) from his stoush-solving years as a labour minister and then as prime minister. The policies he looks back on with the most pride — the treaty process, anti-nuclear legislation, the championing of individual workplace contracts — all had negotiation as their centrepiece. And diplomacy, like chairing government and private sector boards and complex university councils, is also, by definition, about negotiation. Even many of the sometimes surprising but not outrageous views he has picked up over recent years, one suspects, were arrived at through negotiating with the times, as it were, by reading the writing on the political wall.

In a sense, our conversations were negotiations, too, although not in the adversarial sense because this book was a . . . well, I won't say authorised but certainly cooperative venture, which is how we also got the fantastic historical photographs and illustrations sprinkled throughout the text.

Most negotiations are rarely concluded in one sitting. In cases where they are, as American academic Christopher Voss says somewhere, there's invariably stuff left on the table, which is probably why most of the articles that have been produced about Jim Bolger over the years, my own included, have always felt a little slight. There's strength in getting these things down thoroughly. So I hope not *too* much has been left on the table this time.

Later, as I was working through the final draft, Jim said he had found the project challenging in terms of putting what he felt was the right weight on certain events and balancing the distant with the immediate. 'If in any way I've caused some to think more deeply on current issues, then that to me is success,' he wrote. And if I've helped others get to know Jim Bolger better that will be my success.

The Great Helmsman also sent me the words of a famous Native American prayer, which is included in William Kent Krueger's novel *Trickster's Point*:

> O Great Spirit, whose voice I hear in the winds
> And whose breath gives life to everyone, hear me.
> I come to you as one of your many children,
> I am weak, I am small.
> I need your wisdom and your strength.
> Let me walk in beauty, and make my eyes ever
> Behold the red and purple sunsets.
> Make my hand respect the things you have made,
> And make my ears sharp so I may hear your voice.
> Make me wise, so that I may understand what you
> Have taught my people and the lessons you have
> Hidden in each leaf and each rock
> I ask for wisdom and strength, not to be superior to my brothers
> But to be able to fight my greatest enemy, myself.
> Make me ever ready to come before you with clean hands and a straight eye.
> So as life fades away as a fading sunset
> My spirit may come to you without shame.

Acknowledgements

It's a pleasure to thank Jim and Joan for their time over the year. Thanks also to Nicola Legat at Massey University Press for the attention, always beneficial, she gave to getting the idea rolling (and helping to kick it into shape as we proceeded), and to her team — project manager Emily Goldthorpe, editor Anna Rogers and my publicist friend Sarah Thornton for taking the work out of working.

Thanks to Melissa Harsant for assisting with transcriptions. And to my wife, Pamela, for all the usual support and for snapping that nifty back cover photo of Jim and me to go so well with Jane Ussher's smashing portrait on the front.

About the Author

David Cohen is an author and journalist. His work appears regularly in New Zealand and abroad, including commentary and reportage for *The Spectator*, *Arab News* and RNZ. For many years he wrote about higher education for the *Guardian* and local political affairs for *The Christian Science Monitor*. As a reporter, he has interviewed many political leaders, including several New Zealand premiers, the former Malaysian prime minister Mahathir bin Mohamad and the first East Timorese president, Xanana Gusmão.

He is the author of six books, including works of social history, family memoir and music criticism, the last being *Book of Cohen*, a collection of 'late-night essays' about the Canadian artist Leonard Cohen. He has co-authored or contributed chapters to several others. An influential earlier title, *Little Criminals*, was named one of the best books of the year by the *New Zealand Listener*. He lives in Wellington.

Index

A

abortion 41, 91, 101, 108, 111
Africa 177–8
ageing population 111–2, 175
agriculture 184–8, 214–5 *see also* trade, international
All the Shah's Men 227–8
Ammann, Dan 274–5
Anders, Therese 152
Anglo-Iranian Oil 227–8
anti-nuclear policy 13, 130, 145–6, 150, 178–9, 195–209, 219–20, 259–60
Anzac Day lecture 232–5
ANZUS 137–8, 197–8, 209
APEC 206
Ardern, Jacinda 159, 161, 166, 239–41, 253–7
Asia 13, 136, 150
Auckland Freezing Workers Union 67, 69
Australia 133–4, 198

B

Ballance, John 40
Bank of New Zealand 155–6
Bassett, Michael 12–4
Beatson, David 152
Birch, Bill 127, **129**, 154–6
birth rate & population 101–2, 175, 245–6, 251
Bolger, Daniel & Cecilia 26–8, 31–2, 35–8, **39**, 40–1, 53–9, 63, 94–5
Bolger, James Brendan (Jim) **11, 19, 33, 57, 68, 83, 97, 121, 129, 151, 157, 164, 171, 204, 221, 225, 255**
  ambassador 14, 17, 163, 165, 213–35
  childhood & education 10, 17, 20, 51–61
  married & family life 54, 56, 65–6, 78–87, **83**
  in parliament 69, 85–6, 117–39, 143–91, 218
  at Waikanae 239–75
Bolger, Joan 10, 28, 59, 69, 78–87, **83**, **97**, 199, 217–8, **221**
Bolger, Matthew 86–7
Bolger, Stephen & Toni 54, **68**
Bolger: A View From the Top 117, 163
Bolger family 34–5, 62–3, 100–1
The Bolger Years 117
Bolton, John 145–6
BP 227–8
Bracken, Thomas 40, 44
Brash, Don 159
Bridges, Simon 159
Brophy, Joe 58–9
Buckley, Ed 125–6
Burdon, Philip 170
Burns, Jim 12, 127, 152
Bush, Barbara 199–200, 222
Bush, George Herbert Walker 198–200, 220, 222, 242
Bush, George Walker 131, 222, 228, 230, 242
Butler, Lois 84

C

Canada 178
Can Politics be Christian? 106–13
Carmine, Father Eugene 95
Carroll, Charles & John 232
Chathams 32
Chetham, Brendan 222
China 179–80, 246, 257–61, 267–8
Chirac, Jacques 196, 201
Christchurch, mosque attacks 228, 240, 249–51, 253–4
Churchill, Winston 51, 233–5
Churchill: A Life 233–5
Civil War, American 232
Clark, Helen 14, 61, 92, 147, 149, 153, 170, 228, 250, 259
climate change *see* environmentalism
Clinton, Bill 206–7, 219–20, **221**, 230, 242, 263
Clinton, Hillary **221**
Closer Economic Relations 133–4
Collins, Michael 30
colonisation 28, 55, 56, 102–4, 173–4
Commonwealth Heads of Government 203, 205
computers see technology
conservation see environmentalism
Cooper, Whina **57**
corruption 188–9
Country Girls Club 82
Court of Appeal 169–70
Covid-19 18, 20, 105, 156, 160, 240–1, 253, 257, 267–8
Crawford, Roy 61
Cullinane, Peter 108

D

Darroch, Kim 216–7
Davis, Kelvin 244
Davos Economic Forum 272
Dawson family 56, 58, 60
de Cuéllar, Javier Pérez 198–9
defence policies 130, 137–9, 244–5
Depression 59–60, 64, 122
de Valera, Eamon 30
Dewe, Colleen 122–3
Doha Development Round 177, 188
Dominion Post 270
Douglas, Peter 148–9

Douglas, Roger 152–3, 243
Doyle family 27, 31, 35–6
Dutch immigrants 95

E

Eaddy, Robert 152
East, Paul 162–3
Eastern Europe 134–5
economy & economics 13–4, 103, 154–5, 180–1, 186, 257, 267–8 *see also* trade, international
education 61–2, 267
Eisenhower, President 229
Elworthy, Jonathan 252
employment 69, 154, 245, 252–3, 264–5 *see also* unions & industrial disputes
Employment Contracts Act 154
English, Bill 41, 158–9, 165, 170, 256
environmentalism 183–5, 201–5, 252–4, 260, 261, 268–75
Environmental Protection Agency 183–4
European Community & European Union 130, 135–6, 178, 187, 190
euthanasia 108, 111–2
Evening Post 15, 143

F

Fairness and Freedom: A History of Two Open Societies: New Zealand and the United States 215, 216
Farmers' Action Committee 66
Federated Farmers 65
Finlayson, Chris 167
First Gas 273–4
Fiscal Responsibility Act 155–6
Fischer, David Hackett 215, 216
fishing & fisheries 32, 34
Food and Agricultural Organization, United Nations 181
foreign affairs 110, 130–9 *see also* trade, international
forestry 252, 267
France 196–7, 201–2, 203, 207–8
Fraser, Malcolm 133–4
Future Shock 72–3

G

Gair, George 127, 158
GDP 124
General Agreement on Tariffs and Trade 186–7
Georgetown University 232–3
Georgieva, Kristalina 272
Giuliani, Rudy 224
global warming see environmentalism
Good Friday Agreement 30
Graham, Douglas 148–9, **151**, 162, 167
Green Party 165
Greenpeace 201–2, 203
Green Revolution 183
Griffin, Richard 152
Guardian 269
guns & gun control 42, 228–9, 231

H

Hawke, Bob 133–4
Healy, Patrick & Mary 232–3
Hiringa Energy 274
Hobson, William 40, 43
Holland, Sid & Eric 156
Holyoake, Keith 16, 51, 156
homosexuality 41, 87, 123–4, 248
honours system 170
Horo family 55
Hubbard, Jim, cartoon **19**
Hunter, Rachel **225**
Hussein, Saddam see Iraq

I

immigration 101–2, 103–4, 175, 182, 245–7, 249, 262–3
India 173–4, 178–9, 180–2, 189, 191, 258
industrial disputes *see* unions & industrial disputes
inequality *see* social wellbeing
International Court of Justice 201
International Labour Conference 110
International Labour Organization 126–7
International Monetary Fund 186–7, 268, 272
Invisible Urban 274
Iran 145–6, 227–8
Iraq 130–2, 143, 177, 206, 223–4, 229
Ireland 26, 27–47, 29–30, 43, 45–7, 226–7
Irish Times 257
Ishkov, Alexander 32

J

Japan 34, 178, 200, 208–9, 246–7
Johnson, Boris 216–7
Johnson, Lyndon B. 41–2, 230–1
Jones, Bob 130

K

Katherine O'Regan **157**
Kearins, Mick **68**
Kennedy, John F. 40–2, 182–3, 185, 213
Key, John 13, 14, 159, 165, 166, 167, 170, 254, 256
Khashoggi, Jamal 146
Kidd, Doug 148–9
King, Stephen 252
King Country *see* Te Kuiti & King Country
Kinzer, Stephen 227–8
Kirk, Norman 12, 16, 51, 66–7, 119–22, 196, 197
Kiwibank 14, **19**
KiwiBuild 103
KiwiRail 14
Knox, Jim 126–8
Korea 34, 207
Korean War 122
Krueger, William Kent 280
Kruger, Tāmati 167
Kuriger, Anna & Barbara 84
Kuwait 130–1, 206

L

Labour Government & Party 12–3, 14, 15, 64, 69, 119–20, 132, 135, 152–3
Lange, David 51, **121**, 128, 152–3, 197–8, 259
Latimer, Graham 148–9, 167
leadership 146–54, 156–65, 169–72, 218, 265, 271, 279–80
Lewinsky, Monica 213, 219–20
Little, Andrew 159
Local Government New Zealand 18, 20, 267–75
Luther, Martin 96

M

Mahathir bin Mohamad 261
Mahuta, Robert 148–9, **151**
Major, John 205
Mandela, Nelson 46, 152, 203–5, **204**
Māori 28–9, 37, 42, 43, 55–6, 95, 98, 103–4, 120, 169, 226–7, 245–6
  land ownership 55–6, 167–8, 173–4
  Māori Language Week 256
Marilyn Waring: The Political Years 124
market forces *see* neoliberalism
Marshall, John 156
Martin Gilbert 233–5
McHardy, Jack & family 37–8, 64
McKinnon, Don 155–6, 158
McLay, Jim 128, 158
meat industry 65–6, 67, 69, 125–6
media 69, 263–4
Merkel, Angela 104, 262–4
Metro 17
Microsoft 70–5
Middle East 130, 226, 227–8
MMP 13, 154, 169, 264–5
Moore, Mike 12, 16, 51, **121**, 133, 135, 153, **164**
morals *see* values
Mossadegh, Mohammad 227–8
Mother of all Budgets 143–4
Mother Teresa 108
Muldoon, Robert 12, 15, 32, 67, 110, 120, **121**, 127–8, 156, 158, 209
Muller, Todd 21, 159–60
Murdoch, Simon 150–1
Murphy, John 44–5, 46
Myanmar 247

N

National Government & Party 64, 117, 120, 122–3, 127–8
national superannuation 67, 165–6, 254, 256, 261–2
Nehru, Prime Minister 179, 189
neoliberalism 73–4, 154–6, 243–4
Newcastle University 257
New Zealand First 160–1
New Zealand Herald 274
New Zealand Meat Board 125–6
Nigeria 205
Nizami Ganjavi International Center 92
nuclear policy *see* anti-nuclear policy

O

O'Brien, Terence 198–9
OECD 188
Omata 53
Orbán, Viktor 245, 262
O'Regan, Tipene 148–9
O'Reilly, John Boyle 190

P

Pacific region 13, 32–4, 131, 132–4, 137–9, 196, 201–5, 262
Palmer, Geoffrey 12, 153
Parihaka 168, 173–4
Paris Climate Accords 270
Pence, Mike 86
pension see national superannuation
Peters, Winston 160–1, **164**, 272
Phillips, Jock 26
'Picking Up the Chips': The Microprocessor Challenge in New Zealand 70–5
Plummer, Paul 152
politics, funding of 242–3
Pollen, Daniel 26
Pope Francis 98
Pope John Paul II 91, 92, 97, 186
Popper, Karl 144
population *see* ageing population; birth rate & population
Powell, Colin 224
Prendiville, Pat 101
Prime Minister's Department 150–1
Pureora Forest 252
Putman, Robert 163

Q

Queen Elizabeth **171**, 172
Queen Elizabeth 234
quotas see tariffs & subsidies

R

racism 42, 102, 103–4, 110, 190, 230–1, 245–6, 248–51, 249–50, 260–1
Rahotu 53–63
Rainbow Warrior 201–2, 203
Ready Reaction Force 138
Reagan, Ronald 242, 263
referendums 264–5
religions 30, 41, 87, 91–113, 228, 247–50
republicanism 13, 25, 30, 170, 172, 262–3
retirement age *see* national superannuation
Richardson, Ruth 13–3, 79, 143–4, 154–6, **157**
Riddell, Joan 10, 59
Riddiford, Daniel J. 66, 69
Roche, Brian 170
Rohingya people 247
Roosevelt, Franklin Delano 178
Rowling, Bill 153, 218
Russia 32, 34, 131, 134–5, 207–8, 247

S

Sachs, Jeffrey 180
Saro-Wiwa, Ken 205
Saudi Arabia 131–2, 146, 222–6, 229, 248
Saul, John Ralston 235
Savage, Michael Joseph 64, 92
Scandinavia 244–5
Scotland 226–7
Scott, Tom, cartoons **164**, **255**
Scowcroft, Brent 198–9
Sealord 148–9
sexual abuse 96, 98
Shipley, Jenny 14, 15, 92, **157**, 160, 161–3, 218, 250
slavery 109–10, 166, 230, 232–3
Smith, Al 41
Social Credit Party 69
social wellbeing 64, 124, 159, 163, 169, 175–6, 178–82, 185–6, 189, 215, 216, 244–5, 258, 261–2
Somers, Edward 200, 259
South Africa 46, 110, 190, 203, 207, 250
South Pacific Forum 132–3, 138
Soviet Union *see* Russia
Stafford, Edward William 44
Stalin 92
Stewart, Rod **225**
subsidies *see* tariffs & subsidies
superannuation *see* national superannuation

T

Tainui 151, 167, 171
Taking a Global View 130–9
Talboys, Brian 34
tariffs & subsidies 177–8, 180, 186–8, 190 *see also* trade, international
tax 107, 155, 242, 244, 254
Te Arikinui Dame Te Atairangikaahu **151**
technology 70–5, 264–6
Te Kuiti & King Country 54, 66–7, 85, 125–6
Templeton, Hugh 127, 250
terrorism 176, 177, 182, 185, 189, 190, 222–3, 222–8, 228–9
Te Urewera 167–8
Te Whiti o Rongomai 173–4
Thomson, David 127
Thunberg, Greta 268
Thwaites Glacier 269–70
timber 252, 267
Time 272
Tirikatene-Sullivan, Whetu 120
Toffler, Alvin 72–3
Tone, Wolfe 47
tourism 120, 214, 267
trade, international 18, 20, 110, 133–4, 135–6, 150, 176–8, 180–1, 186, 188, 189, 190, 214–5, 219 *see also* agriculture; economy; foreign affairs; tariffs & subsidies
Treaty of Waitangi & settlements 13, 43–4, 148–9, 151, 166–8, 169, 256
Trickster's Point 280
Trump, Donald 99, 145–6, 153, 166, 216–7, 229–30, 242, 248, 249, 258, 263–4, 268
Truth 123–4
Tūhoe 167–8
Turia, Tariana 168

U

unions & industrial disputes 12, 65–6, 67, 69, 125–6, 127 *see also* employment
United Kingdom 130, 135–6, 205, 207–8, 258, 262, 264
United Nations 131–2, 139, 181, 198
United States of America 41–2, 131, 136–8, 177, 182–4, 196–200, 206–7, 213–35, 232, 242–3, 247, 258
University of Waikato, as Chancellor 14, 61–2
Urewera Board 167–8
USS *Truxtun* 196

V

values 84–7, 124
Vatican II 95–6
Vietnam War 122
Voss, Christopher 280
Vote Bolger for Pope **225**

W

Waikato Tainui Settlement Act 171
Waitomo Energy 274
Wall, Michael 128, 152
Ward, Joseph 92
Waring, Marilyn 122–5, 128, 208
Warner, Andrew 180
Washington Post 230
welfare *see* social wellbeing
West Coast Settlement Reserve Lease 55
Wexford 25–47, **33**, 43–7
Wilberforce, William 110
William Gaston 232
Wojtyłła, Karol 91, 92, **97**
women, in politics 118, 120, 122–3, 162 *see also* specific women
Wood, John 167
Wood, Sue 128
Woods, Megan 273–4
World Agricultural Forum 176
World Bank 186–7, 188
World Competitiveness Yearbook 2002 181
World Trade Organization 177–8, 187–8
World War One 122, 233–5
World War Two 63, 122

Y

Young Farmers Club 65, 82, 84

MASSEY
UNIVERSITY
PRESS

First published in 2020 by Massey University Press
Private Bag 102904, North Shore Mail Centre
Auckland 0745, New Zealand
www.masseypress.ac.nz

Design by Kate Barraclough
Cover photographs by Jane Ussher (front) and Pamela Cohen (back)

A catalogue record for this book is available from the National Library of New Zealand

Printed and bound in New Zealand by Printlink

ISBN: 978-0-9951230-2-1
eISBN: 978-0-9951378-6-8